Raising Children With Grit

Library of Congress Cataloging-in-Publication Data

Names: Sanguras, Laila Y., 1977- author.
Title: Raising children with grit : parenting passionate, persistent, and
    successful kids / Laila Y. Sanguras.
Description: Waco, TX : Prufrock Press Inc., [2018] | Includes
    bibliographical references.
Identifiers: LCCN 2018027952 (print) | LCCN 2018032054 (ebook) | ISBN
    9781618218117 (eBook) | ISBN 9781618218100 (pbk.)
Subjects: LCSH: Parenting. | Parent and child. | Discipline of children. |
    Self-control in children.
Classification: LCC HQ755.8 (ebook) | LCC HQ755.8 .S294 2018 (print) | DDC
    306.874--dc23
LC record available at https://lccn.loc.gov/2018027952

Edited by Katy McDowall

Cover design by Micah Benson and layout design by Allegra Denbo
Illustrations by Micah Benson

ISBN-13: 978-1-61821-810-0

Printed in the United States of America.

At the time of this book's publication, all facts and figures cited are the most current available. All telephone numbers, addresses, and website URLs are accurate and active. All pub-
lications, organizations, websites, and other resources exist as described in the book, and
all have been verified. The authors and Prufrock Press Inc. make no warranty or guarantee
concerning the information and materials given out by organizations or content found at
websites, and we are not responsible for any changes that occur after this book's publication.
If you find an error, please contact Prufrock Press Inc.

Prufrock Press Inc.
P.O. Box 8813
Waco, TX 76714-8813
Phone: (800) 998-2208
Fax: (800) 240-0333
http://www.prufrock.com

Raising Children
With
Grit

Parenting
Passionate
Persistent, a
Successful
Kids

Laila Y. Sanguras

PRUFROCK PRESS INC.
WACO, TEXAS

Dedication

To every parent who has questioned her parenting choices, worried that she is messing up her kid, or simply wished for 5 ever-loving minutes alone. You are doing just fine.

Table of Contents

Acknowledgements

I was on a tight deadline for this book in May of 2018, typing feverishly on my laptop. I hadn't even gotten out of bed, let alone showered or brushed my teeth. (Yes, my life is ultra-glamorous.) I announced to my kids that mama was stressed and needed to finish her writing, and I suggested to my husband that he replenish my coffee frequently. My plan worked perfectly for approximately 17 minutes. Then one teenage daughter came in and asked a question I had come to loathe: "What are our plans today?" (Nothing. Mom is busy. Ask your father.) Then another teenage daughter came in to ask yet another dreaded question: "Do we have any breakfast?" (Yes. We have a million options that you will see if you just walk into the kitchen. Ask your father.) My 11-year-old son was next, wondering when we were going to go get the new video game I had promised him. (As soon as mama writes a few thousand words. Ask your father.) Finally, my direction-following 9-year-old son entered the room quietly with a pillow tucked under his shirt so he looked pregnant, a plastic knife under his armpit to look like he had been stabbed, and then proceeded to "die" a slow, yet silent, death in the middle of the room.

This is what parenting is about. Your time (and bed) is no longer your own. You sacrifice every day, but hopefully you also find the humor in your experiences. My kids make me laugh every single day, and I love them deep into my bones. It's because of them that I know what grit looks and feels like. And it's because of them that my world is full of color and sparkles.

Introduction

As soon as I received the contract to write this book, I started to research parenting. I bought a stack of books and read as much as I could. (Thank you, Amazon Prime!) I'm also an actual parent. I'm the biological mom to an 11-year-old boy and a 15-year-old girl. And I'm the bonus mom to a 9-year-old boy, 16-year-old girl, 20-year-old boy/man, and 22-year-old boy/man. If you've been counting, that means I have six children: four boys and two girls—plus a rotation of dogs.

So here I am reading a stack of books, taking notes, and outlining my chapters, and my kids are making me question everything I could possibly know about being a parent. And when I say that, I mean EVERY. SINGLE. THING. I mean, kids are fantastic—except for when they aren't. When you're reading this book, and I'm so appreciative that you are, I just want you to remember that I lost my mind countless times when writing it.

No children were harmed, I assure you, but this has definitely been an exercise in grit. You see, *grit* is the combination of passion and perseverance. I'm passionate about helping teachers and parents navigate the messes our kids create. It's this dream that kept me writing despite my doubts and struggles.

We can also talk about grit in terms of parenting. You are enthusiastic and committed to your children's happiness. You also know that you can't give up on your kids, despite the ways in which they tempt you, so persistence is sort of a requirement. And, of course, there is the point of this book: raising kids who have grit. In Chapter 1, we will explore what it means for children to have grit (and what can happen if they don't have it). Chapter 2 is all about you and how you parent your kids—it was really fun to explore the modern parenting styles that have recently emerged. My goal for Chapter 3 is to help you understand your child and why he behaves the way he does. The next chapter is all about how you can cultivate grit in your children at various stages of development. From there, I spend time sharing ideas for you to help your kids develop the self-discipline necessary for them to be gritty. Chapter 6 is an important one—it's all about how to help your kids find their passions. I give you advice in Chapter 7 for how you can work best with your child's teachers in your quest toward raising a gritty kid. Chapter 8 is about helping your child maneuver through social situations while maintaining passion and perseverance. The final chapter is a discussion of how important it is for you to model grit for your kids.

It's important to remind you that there is no "one thing" we can all do to raise well-adjusted and gritty kids. What works for one of us will backfire for another. But that's okay, because in the process of just trying (and not locking yourself in your bathroom with a warm plate of brownies) you are doing the best you can for your child. It will all work out.

At the end of each chapter is a quote from a song, which I compiled into a "Parenting for Grit" playlist at the end of the book. These are songs that (a) are relevant to our exploration of grit, and (b) are some of my favorites. In addition to the nine songs for the nine chapters in this book, I added a 10th song because one of the words in the title rhymes with "gritty." Now you can't wait to check it out, huh? I hope you love them all!

I end the book with a list of questions that I may not have addressed in other parts of the book. I wanted to tackle these for you in the context of grit. I gathered the questions from friends on social media—I would love it if you would follow me so you can participate next time.

Chapter 1

Grit and the Psychology of Failure

Do you ever worry about what other parents think of you? Are you concerned that your child's teacher wonders what you were thinking when you forgot to send your son to school with a jacket? Are you anxious that your parents are judging your parenting skills when they're around your kids? Well I've got news for you. You are not alone.

I don't know many parents who haven't felt these same doubts and concerns. Parenting is rough. On one hand, we are so scared of messing up our kids that we live in a constant state of worry and fear. And then we're so self-conscious about those fears that we don't share with other parents—especially the ones who seem to have everything figured out.

On the other hand, we face legitimate angst when we hear about school shootings (Sky News, n.d.), the rising rate of childhood anxiety (Bharanidharan, 2018), and whether video games are addictive (Agencies, 2018). Potential threats to our children come at us from all angles, and it feels impossible to keep up, let alone protect them.

Here's the thing. You're afraid to fail. And you're not alone—not only does every parent share this fear, but your children are also afraid to fail. They don't want to let you down, and they feel all kinds of pressure to fit in and succeed at school, with their friends, etc.

You understand that fear of failure—it's also called *atychiphobia*, in case you want to impress your kids with your vocabulary at dinner tonight (Winch, 2013). You've felt your palms sweat and your heart race when you've stood on the precipice of a new adventure. There's also a good chance that you have shied away from taking a risk because the fear of an undesirable outcome was too great. And that's crazy, right?

Because life is full of opportunities and we know that we're bound to be unsuccessful at some point, so why not just go for it? Well, it turns out that there is more to understand about failure than just the physiological effects.

Winner and Loser Effects

Get this. If you failed at something once—just once—you are less likely to try that activity again. For example, let's talk about Cam, your son with a love for nontraditional sports and snack bars. Well, if Cam tries out for the bowling team and doesn't make it, there is a chance that he won't try out again. He knows what it feels like to fail and is averse to feeling that discomfort again. The point is that the *effect* of his failure lasts longer than the actual failure. Think about what this means in terms of your kids—and how it may change your "pick yourself up and try again" speech.

The opposite of this failure effect is called the Winner Effect (Hsu, Earley, & Wolf, 2006), a phenomenon studied by biologists for years. The science boils down to this: Winning heightens and losing diminishes the likelihood of a positive outcome of a later contest. For example, if Cam tries out for the bowling team and makes it, then he is more likely to make the team when he tries out again. His skills have obviously improved because of the season of practice, but he also has a certain confident swagger when strutting through the bowling alley. He knows he's successful, so he continues to be successful. It's a self-fulfilling prophecy!

Fear of Failure

I want to spend some time talking about failure. We're all grownups here and know that it is inevitable, but we also need to fully understand what it means to fail in the context of grit. We have to help our children deal with all parts of life, especially the moments that make them feel like their world is crashing around them. (And if you have teenagers, this happens approximately 14 times a day.) We need to equip our kids with the skills to overcome setbacks so they aren't afraid to take risks.

This fear of failure can be broken down into five responses (Conroy, Willow, & Metzler, 2002):

1. shame and embarrassment,
2. lowered self-worth,
3. uncertainty of the future,
4. losing the interest of significant others, and
5. upsetting significant others.

Conroy and his colleagues developed the Performance Failure Appraisal Inventory (PFAI) to measure each of these responses. Interestingly, most of the items on the instrument assessed how participants interpreted how *others* felt about them and their "failures," not how they personally felt about them. This tells us quite a bit about how we view failure—it's more about our perceptions of what others think of us and not what we think of ourselves. And can't you just imagine that this is amplified in kids?

Much of what we understand about winning and losing comes from research on wild animals. (Yes, the "wild animal" can also symbolize a child.) Okay, so, when an animal is engaged in a contest, it continuously evaluates the costs and benefits of that contest, as well as its ability to fight (Hsu et al., 2006). The effort that the animal expends in the next contest is related to how it feels about the outcome, its capacity as a fighter, and what was lost/gained in the contest. This means that if the animal feels lousy about its performance, it will either resist future contests or will put forth limited effort. It will also decide whether engaging in another contest is worth it based on its cost-benefit analysis.

At the risk of beating the bowling analogy to death, let's transfer what we know about animals to what this means for our kids. For example, if Cam tries out for the bowling team and makes it, but must practice every weekend and is still not as good as his teammates, there is a chance he will stop pushing himself so hard. If he doesn't really care about bowling, he may stop practicing altogether and just endure the rest of the season because he likes the nachos from the concession stand. Essentially, he has decided that the costs are too high compared to the benefits, *and* there is a good chance he won't win his games anyway—because he recognizes that he isn't really that great.

Grit is the combination of passion and perseverance.

At this point, you're either right here with me or you're ready to toss me on the shelf with all of the other parenting "experts." Hang in there with me, please.

Imagine your son Cam at school, in a rigorous—but boring—math class. Cam studies and his grades are decent, but he isn't really pushing himself. As the year progresses, his effort decreases, and then next year he is ready to sign up for a lower level math class. Now, his language arts class is also rigorous, but every day is different and kind of fun. Cam studies and his grades are decent, but he, again, isn't really pushing himself. As the year progresses, his effort increases, and then next year he wants to sign up for a challenging language arts course. The scenarios are very similar. The differences are the costs and benefits. Cam has to study in both, giving up time and energy, but as the benefits multiply, the losses are worth it.

That, my friends, is *grit*. Grit is the combination of passion and perseverance. Grit is what it takes to keep going when you just want to quit. It's the stick-to-itiveness that we want our children to have because we know the importance of not giving up. And we think this for good reason.

Duckworth, Peterson, Matthews, and Kelly (2007) examined the relationships between grit and a variety of variables. Guess what they found? Grit accounted for more individual differences in success outcomes than IQ. That means that grit, a construct that we can help our kids develop, has a greater impact on success than a fairly stable characteristic, like IQ. If you're not super excited by that news, then you should really read that sentence again.

Think of it this way. We can break grit down into parts and provide our children with experiences to cultivate each of those parts. We can help them develop their interests into passions, and we can teach them how to persevere through any challenges they face. We can't do that with IQ—it basically stays the same over time. In fact, we know that grit can be developed because older participants scored higher on the Grit Scale (see Duckworth, 2018) than younger ones. *And* grittier individuals completed higher levels of education and changed careers fewer times than the less gritty (Duckworth et al., 2007).

Let's Talk Science

John Coates (2012), a former stock market trader turned neuroscientist turned author, identified testosterone and cortisol as the hormones responsible for success and failure. As a result of his research on stock market traders in action, Coates found testosterone levels spiked along with financial hikes, while cortisol levels dropped when stocks tanked.

Coates (2012) cited a study in which researchers analyzed the results of more than half-a-million tennis matches. The researchers found that 60% of the players who won their first match won the second match. He concluded that the rush of testosterone generated a cycle of success that extended to other competitive environments (i.e., hockey, chess, etc.; Popova, 2012).

This tells us that, chemically, our bodies are prepared to repeat success after success. And we know that this is also true of failure. Our experiences begin to loop and build upon one another, regardless of whether we are "winning" or "losing." It's important to understand this so that we know how to respond to our children's successes and failures.

It does us no good to tell our kids, "Just get over it," or "It's not that big of a deal."

Failure can quickly turn into rejection, and vice versa. For example, Peter may try to join his peers in a game of basketball at recess, only to be turned away. This rejection that he experienced makes him feel as though something is wrong with him or he is somehow unworthy as a friend. Get this: When we feel physical pain, our brains release opioids to help us deal with what is hurting us (Jiang, 2015). But you know what? The same is true for emotional pain!

A group of researchers at the University of Michigan Medical School ran an experiment to see if our brains respond to emotional pain in the same way (i.e., releasing these opioids into our systems; Jiang, 2015). They recruited participants, hooked them up to a brain scanner, and asked them to look through some fake dating profiles and point out the ones they were interested in. The researchers then gave the whole "It's not you, it's me" speech to the participants and told them that these fake men and women were not interested in dating them. Do you know what happened? The brain scanner detected opioids being released as soon as the rejections started. What's even more interesting is that the participants knew that the dating profiles and the rejections were not even real, yet their brains still responded as if they were.

We can pull two "ah-has" from this. One, Peter's brain would have responded the same way, whether his peers socially rejected him or they pelted him with basketballs from close range. And two, it does us no good to tell our kids, "Just get over it," or "It's not that big of a deal." Their brains are sending them a different (and more powerful) message.

How to Handle Failure

In *You Learn by Living*, Eleanor Roosevelt (1960) wrote, "The purpose of life . . . is to live it, to taste experience to the utmost, to reach out eagerly and without fear for newer and richer experience" (foreword). If we are to live up to the former first lady's advice, we are bound to be let down at some point. To prepare ourselves—and our kids—for the inevitable, we have to figure out how to handle failure.

First of all, failure looks different for everyone. I taught students who thought of failure as a true F, and others called themselves failures if they earned less than an A on a paper. I have friends who get sucked into a downward spiral when they spend too much time on social media, upset that their lives don't live up to the perfection we tend to post online. One of my children slumps into a depressed state when her friends plan a social event without her. The point is that we view our failures in terms of our goals and values. The things we want most are often the things that cause us the most heartache, and there is nothing wrong with that.

As parents, we get ourselves into a pickle when we discount the struggles of our children because they are not important to us. My son gets upset when his videogame avatar dies, which I don't particularly care about, but I'm willing to listen to his story of how it happened (to a point). Each experience, even if it seems trivial to us, is an opportunity for our kids to understand their feelings during difficult times. Let's explore some ways we can do this.

Caroline Beaton (2017) offered three suggestions for how to handle failure.

1. Don't Obsess Over It

We all get caught up in trying to learn from our failures, agonizing over every detail. More times than I can count, I have lain in bed reliving a situation in which I felt less than incredible. No matter how many times I looked at it, the result was still the same: I had let myself or someone else down, and I regretted it.

What you really need to do is recognize that living your best life involves not quite meeting your expectations sometimes, and then focus on how you can move forward.

My family and I have been working hard at paying off debt (we all thank you for buying this book), so we listen to a lot of Dave Ramsey's podcasts. Episode #9389 is called "What You Focus on Is What Happens." Regardless of what Dave discussed on this show, the title tells us a lot. Sure, there is value in learning from your experiences, but that should be a small part of how you deal with failure. What you really need to do is recognize that living your best life involves not quite meeting your expectations sometimes, and then focus on how you can move forward. Better yet, reframe the experience and focus on how it will get you closer to your goals.

As a parent, this means that you need to be open to discussing your child's failures, but you need to resist the urge to harp on them. It isn't helpful. In fact, the shame and misery that comes from wallowing in your child's mistakes can be detrimental to their coping process. The story he tells himself focuses on where he fell short—this story is the same loop that will play in his head when he is in a similar situation in the future. It's almost as if his brain is betraying him, reminding him of the time he crashed and burned previously. Who wants that?

2. Don't Fly Blind

When we are scared, we tend to make one of two choices. We close our eyes and take the leap, or we back away and pursue a different path. Although these options are fine if we are on the edge of a cliff looking down at a vast pool of water, they aren't very healthy choices when we're talking about pursuing passion.

Beaton (2017) suggested that we start by identifying our dreams and then work backward to outline daily goals. Angela Duckworth (2016), the University of Pennsylvania psychologist who brought grit into the limelight with her 2013 TED Talk, described the goal-setting process as a hierarchy. Your dream, or stretch goal, is at the top, and then your smaller goals and daily actions trickle down from there.

Let's take a look at an example of what I'm talking about. Now, if your kids are anything like mine, they have some crazy dreams that may require a miracle and a heap of luck to come true. My 11-year-old son wants to be a professional basketball player someday. He plays on a team now and is one of the most skilled ball handlers I've seen from someone his age. He's fast, hustles 100% of the time, and cheers for his team with exuberance. He's also small for his age, shorter than most of the boys on his team. Now, although I'm not a basketball expert, I recognize that height is a common factor among professional b-ballers. It would be easy for me to steer his interests toward other sports more suited for his stature, but why would I send the message to him that his passion doesn't matter? I wouldn't. Instead, I helped him create his stretch goal hierarchy (see Figure 1).

Another important step is identifying mentors and outside resources that will be helpful in achieving the stretch goal. It is at this step that I want to think about the myriad ways that I can find positive influences for my son as he pursues basketball. For instance, my son would benefit from regularly attending basketball camps and clinics. He could learn a lot from watching local teams play and getting to know the players. His love of the game could be enhanced by finding a young group of kids to help coach.

As part of the goal-setting process, Christine Fonseca (2017) also suggested that we help our kids identify potential barriers to achieving their goals. This is another important step in bringing those stretch goals closer to reality. As you work with your child to identify barriers, it is important to note that these are *potential* obstacles; as with any brainstorm, there are no wrong suggestions. Once your children have named these barriers, they will not be as scary if they do come to fruition (see Figure 2).

A final recommendation from Fonseca (2017) is to articulate the benefits to reaching their goals. Again, by assigning words to feelings, feelings become tangible reminders of why a goal was important in the first place. That way, when your child encounters a barrier or is faced

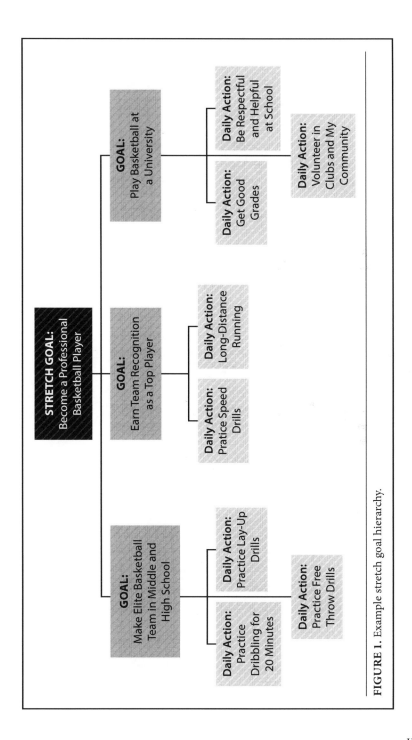

FIGURE 1. Example stretch goal hierarchy.

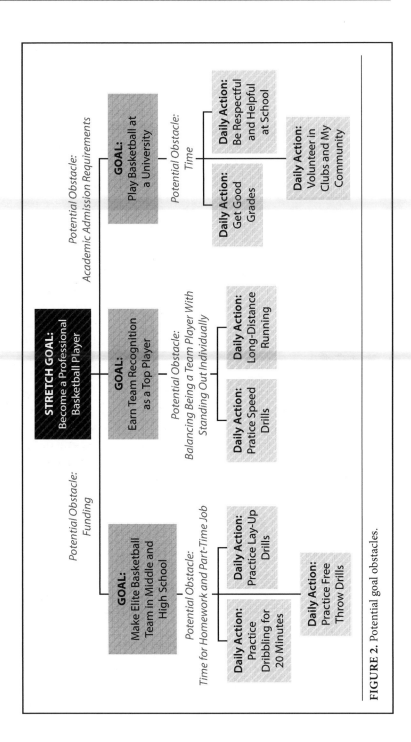

FIGURE 2. Potential goal obstacles.

with a seemingly overwhelming challenge, he can be pulled back to that focused pursuit of his passions.

3. Don't Motivate With Fear

Have you ever stood outside of an important meeting, exhaling to calm your nerves, and whispering to yourself, "It's now or never." Or have you thought to yourself, "If this doesn't work, I'm giving up," or "Don't make a fool of yourself again." I have—over and over again. In some cases, fear is healthy and helpful, but in motivation, fear does not work. It causes our blood pressure to rise and adrenaline to flood our bodies, which are helpful physiological responses when we're running from a rabid dog, but not so helpful when we're building our dreams.

Instead, Beaton (2017) suggested that we celebrate our small successes. By focusing on the small movements toward our stretch goals, we gain momentum that propels us forward to the next achievable step. Perhaps your daughter wants to earn an A in the last semester of her Spanish class after struggling all year. She knows she has a test coming up on verb conjugation and has studied for hours each night. When you kiss her goodbye the morning of the test, don't remind her how important this test is to her final grade. Remind her that by staying committed to her daily actions, she is even closer to her stretch goal. That's it. Then, when the grade comes back, it is not a do-or-die situation. She either did well or she didn't, but regardless, she knows that she is inching toward that A that she wants. You can help her see that test as a reference point for how she can continue moving forward.

Rethinking Success and Failure

As with most parenting issues, rethinking how we view success and failure is easier said than done, right? Manu Kapur (2016) explored a few ways we can think about success and failure differently. First, and what we consider to be most desirable, is productive success. The result of productive success is, obviously, success, but what I want to focus on is the "productive" aspect. If someone experiences productive success, she also learns problem-solving and critical thinking skills. You can think of this as your daughter signing up to take an advanced English course in high school; she has most of the tools necessary to succeed, and will learn transferable soft skills and content throughout the year.

Unproductive success, on the other hand, is when the outcome is favorable, but little knowledge, if any, was gained. If your daughter decided to take an on-level English course because she didn't want to have to work hard, but wanted a high grade, she would likely experience unproductive success. She would earn the grade she wanted, but wouldn't improve her soft skills by much. To this type of success, I want to ask, "What's the point?" and suggest that we just give those students their desired grades and let them go on their way.

Kapur (2016) also explored two different types of failure. The first is *unproductive failure*, which is when there is no learning gained in content and process. This would be if your daughter decided to take a woodshop course as an elective, but had little to no experience. When she walked into class, she realized there was no teacher and she just had to figure out how to design and create projects on her own. By the end of the semester, she may have learned a little, but would not be considered a "successful" woodworker. Additionally, because of her lack of understanding of the field of woodshop, her process skills would also not improve much.

Finally, Kapur (2016) discussed *productive failure*. By now you've probably realized that this is when the outcome is not so desirable, but much is gained by the experience of trying and working through the challenges. If your daughter took woodshop with an instructor and made a clean, yet slightly wobbly, napkin holder in her course, she would have experienced productive failure. Her napkin holder was not going to win any awards, but she learned a great deal about how to problem solve her way through many issues. (By the way, this "daughter" was me, and my mom still uses my napkin holder today.)

So what does this mean for you and your children? First, they should absolutely understand these quadrants of success and failure (see Figure 3). Second, they should be familiar with the language of success and failure. After their experiences, regardless of the outcome, you should be talking about the process and content that was gained. By making this part of your conversations, your children will understand the value in the outcome and how they got there.

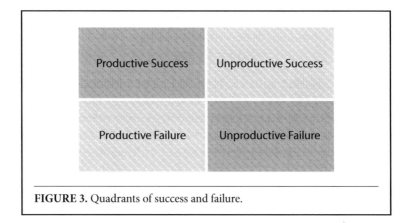

FIGURE 3. Quadrants of success and failure.

And Another Thing

This reconception of success and failure reveals precisely what is wrong with participation trophies. Hopefully you agree that receiving a trophy just for periodically showing up is not a good idea. If you love the notion of recognizing faux achievements, then we should probably (respectfully) part ways because we are fundamentally so different that you will hate me by the end of the book, and no one wants that. Let's break down what an unearned recognition tells a child.

First, the trophy suggests that your child is no different from any other child on the team or in the club. If everyone earns the same recognition regardless of effort, commitment, and passion, it holds no merit. It's like when my friends came to visit me at the hospital after I had my daughter, commenting about my "glow" and how beautiful I looked. Please. I had just survived the most painful and emotional 24 hours of my life. The "glow" was a mix of sweat, tears, and probably some sort of fluid. Who were they kidding? I knew they were just being nice, so I didn't really attach any meaning to their comments. I've seen the Instagram posts of the moms who glow post-birth, and I know I'm not one of them. I would have preferred that we just kept it real, celebrated the miracle of life, and created a plan that would keep my daughter and me alive once the hospital made us go home. Kids are the same.

Think about how you define "well done" and
how you communicate that to your child.

The kid who was the best on the team knows the trophy is a farce and will likely set it next to the other trophies, not giving it another thought. The kid who was the worst on the team also knows the trophy is absurd because he remembers the practices he spent perfecting his cartwheels on the sidelines and the one time he scored in the opponent's goal. He will likely set his trophy on his desk until he replaces it with a recognition that actually matters to him.

Alfie Kohn has spent most of his career studying motivation, and he has interesting thoughts on rewarding children for their behavior (regardless of if the reward is earned or not). Kohn (2005) argued that rewards are indicators of obedience, not a change in behavior. He described a study in which children were rewarded for behaviors that were "nice" toward others. In the experiment, the researchers found that when the reward was removed, the children were less likely to be nice. After all, what was the point?

So, parents, let's take a moment to discuss the bumper stickers that many schools send home with certain students at the end of the semester. You know the ones: "I'm proud of my honor student," and "My child is a top student at XYZ Elementary." Kohn (2005) argued that these bumper stickers suggest that our attention and pride in our children is conditional on specific behaviors. Essentially, the sticker represents how we feel about our children, while sending the message that our feelings are dependent on them earning certain grades or achieving a certain goal. Well, what happens when your child falls short the next semester? Do you scrape the sticker off of your car?

Ask yourself what that sticker represents. Again, does it symbolize obedience and seat time? A monkey could do that, given the right training and some monkey treats. Our schools (and you) have the best of intentions, and you want to recognize your child for a job well done. I just want to encourage you to think about how you define "well done" and how you communicate that to your child.

Why Should We Be Concerned With How Our Children Process Failure?

Whether we recognize it at the time or not, failure makes an imprint on how we process future events. Sometimes our responses are dramatic, and we fall into a depressed state. Other times we may shrug it off and move on. Either way, we don't forget, and how we frame the event in our minds will influence how we feel when faced with a similar situation.

When this happens time and again, our self-esteem is affected, which, in turn, impacts so many areas of our lives. (Now, this is not the part of the book where I am going to encourage you to coddle your child. I'm not advocating that you actually or metaphorically wrap him in bubble wrap to protect him from everything that wants to destroy him. What I have to say is even better. Read on. . . .)

Simply put, *self-esteem* is how you feel about yourself. Do you love yourself like you love others, or do you only see your faults and shortcomings? Brown and Dutton (1995) described self-esteem as the regulation of one's feelings of self-worth (i.e., feeling shame or pride). In their study, they reported some interesting findings. First, they found that participants' self-esteem had nothing to do with whether they were happy or upset after succeeding or failing at a task. But you know what self-esteem did influence? Whether they felt shame or pride. As a parent, this is important for you to know. If your son has his heart set on winning the spelling bee at school but loses, he may shrug it off and happily ask to go out for ice cream. You're thinking to yourself that you sure have raised a resilient kid and tell him to get two scoops! But what you're *not* seeing is what is important. Underneath the chocolate-coated smile is a boy who is questioning himself as a speller, who is anxious about facing his classmates the next day, and who is reliving the embarrassment of having to return to his seat on stage after misspelling "aardvark."

Another finding that Brown and Dutton (1995) reported was that failure had a greater influence on participants with lower self-esteem than those with high self-esteem, while success had the same influence on both groups. This tells us that, in general, children with a higher self-esteem can succeed and fail with minimal impact on their sense of self-worth. You may be wondering why this is. Well, there are several theories that may lead us to deeper understanding.

Individuals with low self-esteem tend to have poor understanding of their strengths and weaknesses (Campbell, 1990). Because they spend so much energy feeling badly about themselves, they struggle to identify what it is that they do well. They tend to look for external feedback to guide and inform them of their strengths.

Another interesting theory is that people with healthy self-esteem manage a failure in one area of their lives by invoking positive self-talk about successes they have had in other areas of their lives (Steele, 1988). Well, you can imagine what happens to people who can't identify other strengths they have. It's a downward spiral.

We have to help our children break the
link between failure and self-worth.

You may be wondering about the point of encouraging our children to pursue their passions, especially big, dreamy passions, if failure is inevitable. After all, life is hard enough without having to determine if your kid has low or high self-esteem and how that manifests itself. Well, one of the most interesting sentences of the Brown and Dutton (1995) article was just tucked into a paragraph almost at the end and addresses that exact thought. They suggested that we have to help our children break the link between failure and self-worth, particularly feelings of worthlessness. Additionally, we need to encourage academic and goal-oriented risk-taking with our children, giving them the tools to identify the benefits of a situation *in spite of* the risks and potential for failure.

The Last Word

It's the eye of the tiger, it's the thrill of the fight
Risin' up to the challenge of our rival.

—Survivor

If we want to raise our kids to be gritty, we must understand success and failure. We need to focus on the process of *doing*, rather than on the outcome. By shifting our perspective, we can help our children keep their self-esteem independent from the outcomes of their experiences. We will also find that we have a lot more in common with our kids if we focus on the process. For example, although we may not know what it feels like to lose a life in a video game, let a soccer ball fly past us into the goal, or fail a sign language exam, we do know what it means to work toward something and be unsuccessful. That connection will really prove valuable as your child encounters future struggles.

Chapter 2

Getting to Know Your Parenting Style

We want the very best for our children, but let's face it. Sometimes we can be a little too enthusiastic or crazy. We know how difficult life can be and want to protect our children from experiencing the same kind of pain. Although our intentions are noble, sometimes we push our kids too far. All of a sudden, we're yelling from the sidelines for our daughter to run faster toward the goal. Or we're enrolling our sixth grader in a weekend SAT prep class. Or we spend our Saturday telling our son to clean his room and then nitpick every detail because he didn't do it how we would have. (Please tell me it's not just me.)

Glasgow, Dornbusch, Troyer, Steinberg, and Ritter (1997) described the beautiful complexity of parenting styles as "constellations of parental attitudes, practices, and nonverbal expressions" (p. 507). Isn't that lovely? Constellations are long-lasting, meaningful, and mysterious—much like parenting. Alone, stars are just stars. But when grouped with others they become constellations, powerful in their symbolism. So together, we are going to tackle these parenting styles, draw meaning from the research, and connect it all to grit.

But first, let me tell you this: No parent is perfect. Yep, that's right. Not the perfectly-coiffed-room mom. Not the dad who coaches his son's baseball team. Not the president of the parent-teacher organization. Not the superintendent of your child's school district. And not this author. So give yourself a break and let's move on.

Traditional Parenting Styles

Before we talk about these first four parenting styles, I challenge you to take the quiz developed by Active Parenting Publishers available at http://www.activeparenting.com/Parents-Parenting_Style_Quiz. It's a good one and will give you a head start in thinking about how you parent. As we discuss different types of parenting, keep in mind that these findings are general and that every child's personality is different, which can result in different outcomes. Furthermore, cultural norms and expectations are also influential, in addition to a million other factors (i.e., socioeconomic level, family structure, weather, presence of ice cream in the home—you get the point).

No parent is perfect. . . . So give yourself a break
and let's move on.

These first parenting styles are the ones we have been talking about since 1967 when Diana Baumrind first started publishing about them. Baumrind conceptualized parenting in terms of demandingness (i.e., how much a parent tries to control a child's behavior) and responsiveness (i.e., the extent to which a parent responds to a child's needs). I've indicated which parenting style is best for cultivating grit, specifically independence and perseverance, with a checkmark, and the others with an X. Keep in mind that none of us fall perfectly into one category and most likely pull from different parenting styles depending on the child, situation, and our moods.

GRITTY Authoritative Parents

Authoritative parents are those who are demanding of their children, but also respond to their needs and requests. They set clear expectations and follow through with consequences. These parents support their children and value their independence. An authoritative parent is one who will limit screen time, but will give her child choice in his weekly chores. She disciplines by using reason and tries to understand why her child is misbehaving at school.

In general, the children of authoritative parents tend to be happy and confident in their abilities to master a task. They are socially well adjusted and do well in school. Additionally, they tend to respond respectfully toward other authoritative figures (e.g., teachers, bosses, etc.). This is important in developing grit because we want our children to understand that they can meet the reasonable demands placed upon them and that they are capable of making their own decisions.

GRITTY Authoritarian Parents

Authoritarian parents are also demanding, but they are not responsive to their children. They expect their children to obey their rules without question. An authoritarian parent is the one who establishes a routine of snack-homework-dinner-bed that his child follows religiously. This parent will not listen to his child's "side of the story" when an issue arises and works hard to keep his child in line. Children of authoritarian parents tend to be withdrawn and will give up and/or become angry when they are frustrated. They tend to do well in school (both academically and behaviorally), but are described as having poor social skills and higher levels of depression (Darling, 1993).

Children of authoritarian parents have difficulty establishing their independence, which causes problems when they are developing their interests into passions. Furthermore, because they tend to give up when frustrated, these children struggle to develop the mental muscles needed to persevere through challenges.

GRITTY Permissive Parents

Permissive parents are responsive to the needs of their children, but do not place demands on them. They avoid confrontation with their children, which often results in lenience and overindulgence. A permissive parent is the one who is friends with her child, who places few expectations of him regarding chores, and asks for the child's input when attempting to create household structure. This may also be the parent who supplies alcohol for parties, excuses a child's disrespectful behavior toward others, and blames the teacher or other children for her child's issues in school.

The children of permissive parents do not display much persistence when faced with a challenge. They are more likely to rebel against rules and will engage in risky behaviors, like underage drinking and drug use. They tend to perform less well in school when compared to other children, but have higher social skills and self-esteem. They also struggle with authority. All of this adds up to a kid with very little grit—you know, the same kid living in his parents' basement, not paying his bills.

GRITTY Neglectful Parents

Neglectful parents are neither supportive nor demanding of their children. They take care of their children's physical needs, but tend to be indifferent otherwise. Children with neglectful parents are at the greatest disadvantage. They struggle academically and socially. They don't know how to self-regulate their behavior and cannot see the connection between actions and consequences. They also struggle to form relationships with others because they haven't seen this modeled within their families.

The children of neglectful parents struggle to develop grit that extends beyond having their physical needs met. They demonstrate the perseverance necessary to survive, but because this is their primary goal, there is little room for developing passion and persistence in other areas.

Modern Parenting Styles

GRITTY Free-Range Parent

The free-range parenting movement began when Lenore Skenazy allowed her 9-year-old son to find his way home on the subway. In 2008, she was dubbed "America's Worst Mom" by the media, which led to a flurry of attention. The mission of the Free-Range Kids website (developed by Skenazy) is "fighting the belief that our children are in constant danger from creeps, kidnapping, germs, grades, flashers, frustration, failure, baby snatchers, bugs, bullies, men, sleepovers and/or the perils of a non-organic grape" (Free-Range Kids, 2008–2018). Now, when I first heard this term, I thought it was similar to a permissive parent, but this is not the case. Skenazy described free-range parenting as a commonsense approach, and she suggested that parents keep their children safe without protecting them too much from life.

A free-range parent allows her child to walk to the park alone or with a friend. She does not stand in between her child and failure. She teaches her children to use public transportation or ride bikes through the neighborhood. She models how to talk to strangers, so that they aren't a source of danger, but a part of their community.

GRITTY   Conditional Parents

A conditional parent is one who holds something back from her children as a way of controlling them. You might even call it bribery. Have you ever told your child, "If you clean your room, I'll take you to the movies," or "I will give you $5 if you get an A on your biology exam." Just me? I've been on the giving and receiving end of these bribes, and the research is clear: Bribery is ineffective as a parenting strategy.

When we offer a gift to someone for completing an activity, we are sending the message that the task is so undesirable that one would only complete it if a prize were attached. Do you remember learning about classical conditioning in your psychology courses? Essentially, the theory suggests that we learn a response to a stimulus when that behavior is reinforced. In its simplest form, it's like telling your child you will give her a cookie after she sorts her dirty clothes. After you repeat this stimulus/response pattern enough times, your daughter will expect a cookie every time she sorts her dirty clothes. You can't take away the cookie if you want her to continue sorting her clothes.

Alfie Kohn has written about the use of bribes in parenting and teaching for years. In his 2005 book, *Unconditional Parenting: Moving From Rewards and Punishments to Love and Reason*, he explained that parents kid themselves by thinking they are rewarding their children out of love. It's not love; it's control. He argued that parents should offer unconditional love to their children so that we are sending the message that we are proud and love them regardless of their accomplishments and in spite of their failures.

GRITTY Tiger Parents

The term "Tiger Mother" gained momentum in Amy Chua's (2011a) book, *Battle Hymn of the Tiger Mother*. The tiger parent is strict and demanding. She assumes that her child is strong and can handle sharp criticism about anything—her weight, her grades, her hair. The tiger parent places high demands on her child and believes that if the child does not reach those expectations, then the child did not work hard enough. Additionally, the tiger parent presumes to know what is best for her child; therefore, input about what club to join and what classes to take is unnecessary. The parent will decide, and that's that.

Chua, a self-proclaimed tiger mom, began a 2011 *Wall Street Journal* article by describing a variety of activities her daughters could not do: watch television, get a grade lower than an A, and attend a sleepover. She argued that her parenting style may seem harsh, but she (and many Chinese parents) raised her daughters to be mathematical and musical prodigies. To those who critique her, Chua said, "But as a parent, one of the worst things you can do for your child's self-esteem is to let them give up. On the flip side, there's nothing better for building confidence than learning you can do something you thought you couldn't." That sounds a lot like grit, just wrapped up in a cold, spiky package.

GRITTY Helicopter Parents

A wave of research was published that linked parent involvement to everything we want for our children: academic success (Hara & Burke, 1998; Shaver & Walls, 1998; Steinberg, Lamborn, Dornbusch, & Darling, 1992), healthy relationships (Dekovic & Meeus, 1997), positive sense of self (Armsden & Greenberg, 1987; Cripps & Zyromski, 2009), and low risk of engaging in deviant behaviors (Griffin, Botvin, Scheier, Diaz, & Miller, 2000; Patterson, DeBaryshe, & Ramsey, 1989). And what do we do when something is good? We do it *more* because that must be even better, right? Nope. It doesn't take long to move from a well-intentioned parent to the loony one who serves an example of how not to parent.

The term "helicopter parent" came onto the scene when Haim Ginott (1988) recounted a teen's description of his mother in his book, *Between Parent and Teenager.* She was hovering. Foster Cline and Charles Fay (2006) made the term even more popular in their book, *Parenting With Love and Logic.* Cline and Fay pointed out the irony of helicopter parenting. From the outside, it looks like she is the mom of the year, and her child may be effusively giving her hugs and kisses when she brings her project up to the school at the last minute or gets her out of detention. (I'll admit, I've been envious of my neighbors who had the ability to drop everything and go tend to their children's needs at school. I was stuck at work, and my child was stuck at school without a sweatshirt, which meant he couldn't go outside for recess. I was not lavished with hugs and kisses. I wasn't lavished at all. But let me assure you that I snapped out of my jealousy pretty quickly when I realized how absurd it all was—and when my kid remembered his sweatshirt on his own the next day.)

Helicopter parenting is also called "overparenting."

In 2014, the phenomenon of helicopter parenting garnered the attention of academics when a group of researchers developed a 15-item Helicopter Parenting Instrument (HPI; Odenweller, Booth-Butterfield, & Weber). And let me tell you, when psychologists decide they want to measure something, that's when you know it's kind of a big deal.

The HPI was designed for children to take and rate their parents' involvement. Some of the items are "My parent tries to make all of my major decisions," "My parent feels like a bad parent when I make poor choices," and "If my parent does not do certain things for me (e.g., doing laundry, cleaning room, making doctor appointments), they will not get done" (p. 425). You can imagine how these items can effectively measure the involvement of a parent in a child's life.

Helicopter parenting is also called "overparenting." You've seen it a thousand times. It's the parent who intervenes in conflicts on the playground in an effort to smooth things over. It's the parent who calls their college-age child multiple times a day to ask about homework, what he ate for lunch, and whether he is doing his laundry. This parent is heavily invested in whether the child gets good grades, makes the best soccer team, gets the choir solo, and has friends to play with on the weekends—and will intervene and remove obstacles to make sure these things happen. Again, in isolation, these behaviors aren't awful. I mean, you are just showing you care by acting this way, right?

Well, it turns out that researchers have found that this hovering can have negative effects on a child's development. In their study on 268 Millennials (ages 18 to 25), Odenweller, Booth-Butterfield, and Weber (2014) reported several positive relationships between helicopter parenting and some qualities we don't really want in our children:

- **Neuroticism.** Individuals with higher scores on the neuroticism scale tend to experience more emotional stress, depression, and anger than others (McCrae & Costa, 2008).
- **Interpersonal dependency.** People with high scores on this scale rely on others for validation and can feel rejected or anxious when they do not receive their desired affirmations (Blatt, 2004).
- **Lack of coping skills.** Those who measure low in coping skills have difficulty responding to stressful situations effectively (Lazarus & Folkman, 1984).

Consider what you know about helicopter parenting at this point. And now let's discuss how each of those traits are measured. The relationship between them and overparenting will make a lot of sense to you, regardless of the age of your children.

A valid scale to measure neuroticism is the Neuroticism-Extroversion-Openness (NEO) Inventory developed by Costa and McCrae (1992). On the 12-item subscale, you would see items like "Sometimes I feel completely worthless," and "I see myself as depressed." You might also think of a neurotic individual as being self-critical, insecure, or overly sensitive. Can you imagine how a helicopter parent with the best of intentions could develop these traits in her children? By stepping in and handling all issues, the parent sends the message to the child that he is incapable of handling things himself.

The 17-item subscale of the Emotional Reliance on Another Person on the Interpersonal Dependency Scale (Hirschfeld et al., 1977) informs us as to how interpersonal dependency manifests itself. For example, the subscale includes items like "Disapproval by someone I care about is very painful to me," and "I have always had a terrible fear that I will lose the love and support of people I desperately need" (p. 613). Now, it's critical to pay attention to the word choice of these items. The last item uses "desperately need" as a descriptor of the important people in the participant's life. As an infant, "desperate need" is appropriate, but that should lessen as the child develops. The issue here is that helicopter parents don't provide their children with enough space to move from dependent to independent.

Sinclair and Wallston's (2004) Brief Resilient Coping Scale (BRCS) includes items like "I look for creative ways to alter difficult situations," and "Regardless of what happens to me, I believe I can control my reaction to it" (p. 98). Well, let's think about what happens when a parent steps in to handle every conflict in a child's life. Those coping skills don't develop, and the child becomes overly reliant on others to clean up his or her messes. Who wants that?

And if that isn't enough to convince you *not* to hover, you should know that helicopter parenting typically does not result in gritty kids. To develop grit, our children need to be exposed to challenges and then figure out how to overcome them. Well, if you are your kid's "fixer," then there aren't many meaningful challenges available to overcome.

GRITTY Lawnmower or Snow Plow Parents

A lawnmower parent has a lot in common with a helicopter parent; however, instead of hovering overhead to intervene at any point, this parent is out in front of the child, eliminating obstacles before the child even knows what is going on. (Just take a guess as to how this impacts the level of grit your child will develop. Spoiler alert: It's in the negative.)

Here is where things get *cray-zy*. Katherine Martinko (2015) published an interesting article on the dangers of overparenting. Would you believe that job recruiters reported that parents submitted a resume for their child? That parents contacted these recruiters to complain when their child was overlooked for a job? That parents went to interviews with their child? Seriously. It happened. Let's not, people. Let's allow our children to grow up. Let's provide them with opportunities to evolve, whether it's through failure or success.

GRITTY Icebirg Parents

Basking in reflected glory (BIRG) is a term to describe a phenomenon you see everywhere crowds gather: in football stadiums (Cialdini, Borden, Thorne, Walker, Freeman, & Sloan, 1976), middle school cafeterias (Dijkstra, Cillessen, Lindenberg, & Veenstra, 2010), and presidential elections (Miller, 2009). It's the process of associating oneself with those who are successful. When your team wins, you win. When you hang out with the popular crowd, you are popular. When your candidate succeeds, you do as well. (In case you were wondering, the opposite of BIRGing is CORFing, or cutting off reflected failure. Fascinating, right?)

An Icebirg parent (misspelling is intentional) is one who not only sticks the "My child is an honor student" sticker to her car, but also insinuates that her child is better than those who didn't make the honor roll (Kohn, 2005). Furthermore, the Icebirg parent wants everyone to know how *she* contributed to the success of her child. The bumper sticker isn't really about the pride she feels for her daughter's hard work; it's actually about how hard the mom worked to get her child on the honor roll—all of the tutors she hired, the drives to and from school, etc. Her bragging

is excessive, quite annoying, and tied to her sense of self in an unhealthy way (not to mention the messages she sends her child).

As I'm sure you've guessed, this parenting style is not ideal for cultivating grit in your child. Your interests have likely been imposed on your child, and, because her success is cemented to your self-esteem, she has had few opportunities to struggle.

GRITTY Bulldozer Parents

A bulldozer parent takes things just a step further, with slightly different motives. In addition to hovering and being overly involved in his children's lives, this parent pushes himself into the life of the child. He hangs out with the child and her friends. He wants to know about his daughter's classes, but more so that he can vicariously live through her. Think of the bulldozer as the method the parent uses to clear the obstacles from his child's path, but also the way he pushes himself into the center of his child's life (#nothealthy). It's a rare case that a bulldozer parent raises a gritty kid.

Interestingly, Martinko (2015) also provided us with some warning signs to let readers know if they have dipped a toe (or more) into the world of overparenting. Here are my interpretations of these signs. I had some fun considering fictional characters that align with each archetype. Enjoy! Take a healthy look at yourself to see which roles you are playing with your child.

1. **Marie Barone (*Everybody Loves Raymond*; Codependent).** Do you have a hard time enjoying yourself when your child is not present? Are you anxious about what he or she is doing? Do you miss him or her to the point that you cannot enjoy yourself without him or her?

2. **Mr. and Mrs. Dursley (*Harry Potter*; Overindulger).** Do you spoil your child? Do you have an unhealthy image of what "enough" looks like? Have you fallen into the trap of trying to keep up with Joneses? Or maybe you are the Joneses?

3. **Kristina Braverman (*Parenthood*; Lobbyist).** How do you handle it when your child has a conflict with a teacher? Do you

e-mail the baseball coach about playing time? Do you call your child's employer to tell him that he is sick and won't make it to work?

Think of the bulldozer as the method the parent uses to clear the obstacles from his child's path, but also the way he pushes himself into the center of his child's life (#nothealthy).

4. **Paul Blart (*Mall Cop*; Security Guard).** Do you prohibit your son from participating in sports because it's too dangerous? Or in the school musical because it's too feminine? Do you allow your child to roughhouse with friends or do you step in to stop it?

5. **Lily van der Woodsen (*Gossip Girl*; Overhelper).** Do you write your child's homework for her? How many trifold displays have you created on your own? Do you spoil your child, giving him everything he wants and covering for him when he gets in trouble?

6. **Ms. Benson (*iCarly*; Germaphobe).** Do you avoid taking your kid to places where he might get dirty while playing? Are you over-the-top with the hand sanitizer?

7. **Erica Sayers (*Black Swan*; Watchdog).** Do you have cameras in your house to monitor what your children do while you aren't home? Do you accompany your teen daughter and her friends at the mall, following them closely?

8. **Mrs. Bennet (*Pride and Prejudice*; Social Director).** Are you overly concerned with padding your child's resume with extra-curricular activities? Do you fill your weekends with playdates and appointments so that your child doesn't have any down-time? How do you respond when your child says that he is bored?

9. **Beverly Goldberg (*The Goldbergs*; Praiser).** Do you advise your child to take an easier class in school so that he will earn an "A" instead of taking the chance on a lower grade? Do you have (and wear) a t-shirt that lists all of your child's accomplishments?

Although Martinko's (2015) signs provided us with a checkpoint, they do not lay out the absolute rules of parenting. You may need to be the security guard and tell your daughter that she is not leaving the house wearing that top no matter how many tears she sheds. Or you might need to be the social director for your son who is at a new school and struggling to make friends. You also might need to make certain decisions for the safety of your child. Remember that you know best and that we aren't here to judge you.

The thing about parenting (and the reason writing a parenting book is so completely difficult) is that there are very few hard lines separating what to do and what not to do. Sure, we've got the basics down—feeding, sheltering, clothing—but it's all of the other stuff that keeps us up at night wondering if we are ruining our children.

☑ GRITTY Consultant Parents

Cline and Fay (2006) argued that the consultant parenting style, built upon their Love and Logic principles, is the most effective. The consultant parent provides his children with choices, but these choices have limits based on the development of the child. This parenting style evolves as the child develops (which is why it's important to read Chapter 4 of this book), but it centers on guiding children through life by asking questions and offering choices.

Consider Cline and Fay's (2006) idea of affordable prices to learning. They illustrated how much simpler it is for our children to learn from their mistakes "cheaply" when they are children as opposed to the "expensive" penalties as an adult. This is exactly why schools that offer dual enrollment in high school and junior college are doing a great service for students. It's ideal to provide opportunities for kids to stretch themselves while they have a security net below them.

Think back to when I earlier described my son having to miss recess because he forgot his sweatshirt. Now, my son is all boy and *lives* for recess. He and his friends have an ongoing football game going and some sort of points system for every day. It was crushing to him that he couldn't play outside. And it was heartbreaking to me that I had to decline his tearful begging over the phone to bring him some outerwear. Even though it was hard to listen to him cry and know that this was probably going to ruin his day, my choice was made for me. I work too far from his school to bring him anything quickly, so I don't get the satisfaction that I made a smart parenting move.

However, I'm going to give myself a small pat on the back. Even though my choice was forced, I did the right thing. He missed recess, which he forgot about by the time he got home, and he remembered his own sweatshirt the next day. He learned that his actions have definitive consequences and that his choices will determine what those consequences are. My hope is that this will translate to other areas of his life when he gets older. Instead of missing recess, forgetting to pay a bill as an adult can result in getting his water shut off, which is a serious pain. That is the same lesson, but a much less affordable price to learning (#score1formom).

What Are We Afraid Of?

Ummm, everything. Parenting is so scary. We literally have a human being to keep alive. Beyond that, we have the responsibility of raising someone who is kind and responsible and a contributor to society and a million other things. Alfie Kohn (2005) outlined six fears we face as parents. As we walk through these, notice that you are not alone in feeling scared. We've all been there, and it doesn't look like we're getting out anytime soon.

1. **Fear of parental inadequacy.** When you are faced with a situation and don't know how to handle it, what do you do? Some

of us give over the control to our kids—that way, if things don't go well, it's all on them. Others take absolute control and leave no room for negotiation. Oftentimes we end up parenting how we were parented, unless we have a strong aversion to it, which leads us to operate on the complete opposite end of the spectrum. Consider Janie, who was raised by a very strict father and goes on to overindulge her child because she doesn't want him to feel stifled and invisible like she did growing up.

Reassurance: You know more than the tiny human who seems to run your life. Make the best decisions you can and move on.

2. **Fear of powerlessness.** A fear of powerlessness manifests itself as stubborn stand-offs between you and your child. Have you ever told your son that he could not play outside until he cleaned his room, and then days went by with him inside, driving everyone crazy? So then you're caught in a showdown and either have to retreat and give up power, come up with a compromise, or hold firm and possibly lose your mind. Just me?

Reassurance: Changing your mind or ultimatum—when done with a legitimate reason—does not make you a bad parent. It makes you a human being who evolves with the situation.

3. **Fear of being judged.** When my daughter was a toddler, we traveled to California to visit my parents. My mom told me at one point, "You're much softer than I was as a parent." I spent an irrational amount of time analyzing her sentence. Was "softer" good or bad? I respected my mom, so should I try to be more like her? Was she disappointed in my softness? Once you allow that loop in your brain to start, comparing yourself to every other parent, you are bound to feel inadequate.

Reassurance: All of us are flying blind, and you are not alone. You know your child best and can make educated decisions about how to raise him appropriately. Be confident in that.

4. **Fear for our children's safety.** I was terrified the first time I let my son ride his bike to his friend's house. His friend lived a few houses down and—get this—across the street. My kid was going to have to *cross the street*. Well, I let him do it. I watched out the window, peeking through the blinds so he wouldn't see me (because if he did see me that would mean he wasn't watching for traffic on our cul-de-sac, and then I would have known he wasn't ready for this responsibility). I texted with his friend's mom to make sure he arrived safely and then held my breath when she told me he was riding his bike back to my house.

Reassurance: Your child needs independence so that he can develop a strong sense of self. As he gets older, things will get scarier, so you need to adopt some calming techniques to get you through it.

5. **Fear of babying.** When you are making decisions about your children, make them because it is in their best interest, not because the most recent parenting article told you what to do. If your 3-year-old still climbs in bed with you when she gets scared, that's okay. You don't need to force her onto the floor because you're worried your comforting snuggles will lead to her sleeping with you when she's a teenager.

Reassurance: If you think through your decisions, they are often correct. Consulting "experts" can be helpful, but you have the final say in what you deem appropriate.

6. **Fear of permissiveness.** Sometimes we make decisions because we want to appear firm and confident in our choices, but then we actually seem to go against our beliefs. My teenage daughter regularly wails about my crazy rule that I need to meet anyone who takes her away in a car. This means that I want to look into the eyes of the mom, the friends, the boy who pulls into my driveway. My daughter thinks I'm completely unfair, which has resulted in her missing out on some activities with her friends. I have a choice, then, of how to deal with her when she's "stuck" at home with me. She can mope in her room (which she does), but then I can also make her some ice cream or let her pick the show on television. A critic may see me as being a softie (maybe my mom was right), but my goal here is for her to remember that I love her tremendously.

Reassurance: You can be firm and loving, silly and an authority all at the same time.

The Final Word

I'm not afraid
To take a stand
Everybody
Come take my hand
We'll walk this road together

—Eminem

Clearly there are a thousand ways to be both a good and a bad parent, but it boils down to this: Set firm and loving limits. Encourage your child and be someone she can turn to in times of crisis, but remember that you are not her friend. Take time to contemplate how you will handle potential issues before they happen so that you react with her best interests in mind. Give yourself a break when you mess up, and remember that each day is a new opportunity to get it right.

Chapter 3

Understanding Your Child's Personality

Robert McCrae and Paul Costa (1997) wrote an article titled "Personality Trait Structure as a Human Universal." Up until this point, social scientists explored personality in terms of its diversity among varying populations. But with this article, McCrae and Costa began the validation process of their five-factor model of personality across cultures. These traits are often referred to as the Big Five and include neuroticism (versus emotional stability), extraversion, openness to experience, agreeableness (versus antagonism), and conscientiousness (see Figure 4).

The results of this next study are going to *blow your mind*. Are you ready? The Big Five traits are influenced quite a bit by genetics (Jang, Livesley, & Vernon, 1996). This trio of researchers studied 123 pairs of identical twins and 127 pairs of fraternal twins. They found that more than 60% of the variance in scores on the Openness scale could be explained by genetics. That's a lot, y'all. The next highest explanation of the variance was Extraversion at 53%. Approximately 40% of the variances in the remaining three scales were explained by heritability.

Another influence Jang et al. (1996) examined was environment. This makes sense, right? How much can we (i.e., the parents) influence our children's personalities? Well, it turns out very little. The researchers studied shared and nonshared environmental influences. Shared environment refers to the characteristics of the environment that are common for all family members (i.e., beliefs of the parents, socioeconomic status of the family, etc.). Nonshared environment encompasses everything that can be different for children from the same family (i.e., birth order, friends, etc.). Jang et al. found that nonshared environmental fac-

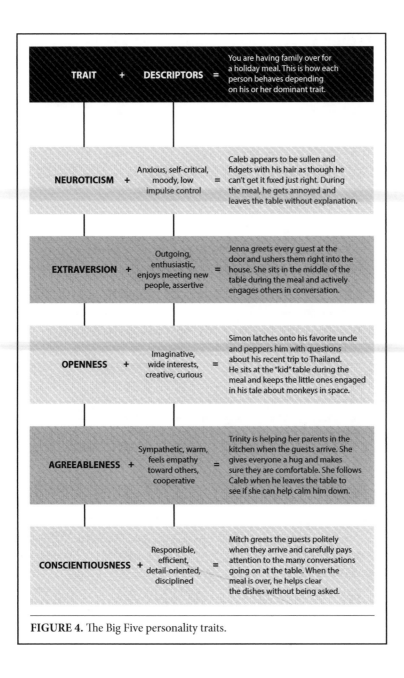

FIGURE 4. The Big Five personality traits.

tors had a much greater influence on personality than the shared. Have you ever wondered why two kids from the same family can be raised the same, but grow up to be so different? Welp, this is why.

It's Hard Out Here for a Kid

Stress is an emotion that we all feel, particularly as the responsibilities of life start piling up. And we all deal with that stress differently. I've been known to go for a long run, call my mom, or eat an entire box of Cheez-Its—even the teeny, tiny crumbs at the bottom of the bag.

It's important for our children to understand how their brains and bodies respond to stress. Fonseca (2017) developed a checklist for her readers as a tool to identify symptoms of their responses to stress (see Figure 5). It's such a great tool!

First of all, the checklist identifies behaviors that aren't exactly negative responses to stress, like the increased need to be with others. We know that stress is positive (also called eustress) when we feel exhilarated and proud once the stressor is removed, like after the dinner party you planned was a wonderful success or you are asked to speak at an event and participants tell you how much they appreciated your words of wisdom. It's important that we use this checklist as a way to connect with our children. Talk about the stressors in your life, both positive and negative.

It's important for our children to understand how their brains and bodies respond to stress.

Second, by helping our children identify their negative responses to stress (also called distress), we can help them regulate those responses. For example, if your son reports that he has difficulty breathing before a big test, you can share meditative breathing techniques to help him cope. The important thing to remember is that we all experience distress—the key to keeping yourself from a Cheez-It incident is knowing how to effectively cope.

This is also the key to developing grit. Perseverance boils down to this: When things get hard, you don't give up. You might need to step

How I React to Stress

Part 1

Directions: Check the box for each symptom of a typical stress response you demonstrate.

❑ Need to be alone	❑ Dry mouth	❑ Tense muscles
❑ Irritability	❑ Grinding teeth	❑ Confusion
❑ Trembling limbs	❑ Increased feelings of courage	❑ Increased urge to call a friend or talk to my parents
❑ Heightened or reduced attention	❑ Blushing, heart palpitations	❑ Increased need to be with others
❑ Emotional upheaval	❑ Neck, shoulder pain	❑ Reduced productivity
❑ Rapid/mumbled speech	❑ Cold or sweaty hands and feet	❑ Increased urge to take action
❑ Memory problems	❑ Headaches, jaw pain	❑ Highly focused attention
❑ Cool skin/ dry mouth	❑ Difficulty breathing	❑ Urge to help others
❑ Difficulties learning new information	❑ Changes in appetite and sleep patterns	❑ Increased excitement or anticipation
❑ Difficulty making decisions	❑ General fatigue or body aches	❑ General feeling of unease

FIGURE 5. Stress reactions checklist. From *Letting Go: A Girl's Guide to Breaking Free of Stress and Anxiety* (p. 17), by C. Fonseca, 2017, Waco, TX: Prufrock Press. Copyright 2017 by Prufrock Press. Reprinted with permission.

aside to take some deep breaths, pause a moment to regain clarity, or talk with someone. But again, you don't quit. Gritty people don't see giving up as an option. They may problem solve or shift their focus to something else, but they do not give up because something is hard. This is how we want our kids to view their experiences.

It's Time to SWOT

SWOT is an analysis commonly used in organizations, but it clearly applies to helping our children understand themselves a little better. SWOT stands for Strengths, Weaknesses, Opportunities, and Threats (Mind Tools Content Team, n.d.). You can do a SWOT analysis with your child or ask her to do it on her own. It's a really valuable tool that I think you will love.

1. **Strengths:** What do you see as your strengths? How would your teachers, friends, and family describe your strengths? What achievements make you proud? What are your values?

2. **Weaknesses:** What are the weaknesses you see in yourself? How would your teachers, friends, and family describe your weaknesses? What do you avoid doing because you don't feel confident in yourself? What are your negative habits?

3. **Opportunities:** Who do you know (or who do your parents know) who can help you achieve your goals? What are connections that your family and friends have? What path do you have available to you because of your circumstances?

4. **Threats:** What are the obstacles you face when pursuing your goals? Do you have any weaknesses that can turn into threats? Do you feel in competition with others?

I encourage you to do your own SWOT analysis and have an honest discussion with your child about what you found. It can provide a way for you both to understand one another a little better. Plus, you are the perfect model for your child to emulate when you're asking her to be introspective. Then go out for ice cream after!

Let's Talk Perfectionism

Were you ever a quiz taker when you were younger? I remember doing every quiz that I could find in my monthly issues of *Teen Bop*, *YM*, and *Sassy*. I was dying to know if I was a better match for Corey Haim or Corey Feldman, or how much I really believed in "girl power." (I should tell you that I was very much a teenybopper in middle school, but I thankfully grew out of it. There's hope for your kids, too.) Perhaps as an adult, you've taken a test to see which Harry Potter house you belong to or which dog breed best matches your personality. Just me? Okay, moving on.

The point is that there is little to no evidence to suggest that these tests have any sort of measurement validity. They won't stand up in court, and you can easily manipulate the results based on your responses. (But I'll tell you—I would love to know which lawyer is defending his client with the shaking of his fist, bellowing, "But my client is from the house of Gryffindor!") Despite the lack of soundness in these instruments, they do inform us of what items the test's author believes can measure that particular construct. You can read them and pretty easily put together the profile of the perfect match for Corey Feldman (not me).

Well, Psychology Today offers its readers tests on pretty much everything, including perfectionism (see https://www.psychologytoday.com/us/tests/personality/perfectionism-test). You can take the test, and the site will provide you with an overall perfectionist profile. You can even pay a fee to get a more detailed breakdown of your results. I'll share some of the items with you so that you can get an idea of what perfectionism is all about (Psychology Today, 2018). (I've adapted them to fit a child.)

- I would rather work alone instead of in a group because I can do it best.
- My work is never good enough for my parents.
- I need to be praised by my teacher to know that I'm good enough.

You get the idea. In a perfectionist's mind, there is little room for error. In fact, Fonseca (2017) suggested that a perfectionist's brain has a mantra that solely focuses on mistakes and weaknesses, completely undermining even a hint of success. It takes focus and fortitude to hush that mantra—after all, how could your brain be wrong?

Well, for a perfectionist, there are plenty of opportunities for failure. Let's break down perfectionism even further into parts so that we can really understand what's going on.

First, there is self-oriented perfectionism (Stoeber, Kempe, & Keogh, 2008). Within this framework, individuals feel the need to be perfect and highly value perfection as a quality. Perfectionism can also be socially prescribed, which means that individuals want to live up to the high standards of others and that they will only be accepted if they meet these standards. You'll notice from Figure 6 that the facets of perfectionism are not mutually exclusive. It's entirely possible that your child can be overcome by the importance of being perfect while also believing that you, her parents, will only be proud of her if she meets your high standards.

You probably already figured this out, but self-oriented perfectionism is considered to be healthier than socially prescribed perfectionism (Campbell & Paula, 2002; Enns & Cox, 2002). That makes sense, right? If you decide that you are going to try to beat your personal time on a half-marathon, you will be less anxious about running than if your coach tells you this is something you must do. However, even though one type of perfectionism is "healthier" than the other, it is generally accepted that perfectionism is not a quality we want for ourselves or our children.

But wait, there's more.

Those of us who are "perfectionist-striving" experience more pride after success than other types of perfectionists (Stoeber, Kempe, & Keogh, 2008). But get this. Those of us who believe in conditional acceptance typically don't experience pride after success. Why do you think that is? Well, it's because we aren't doing "it" for ourselves—we're doing it for others. That bar of success continuously changes if someone else is in charge of it, so we are running a race with no finish line. How can you possibly feel pride if you never feel like you've reached an end point, like you haven't had the opportunity to feel successful?

And one more thing. People who are perfectionists tend to feel more shame after failure than those who are not. And that, my friends, is why we need to help our children overcome their perfectionistic tendencies.

Do you remember feeling shame as a child? Tap into that feeling for a moment. Maybe you retreated into yourself. Perhaps you lashed out at those around you or you ran away. When we are put into experiences where we are embarrassed about what we've done or how we see our-

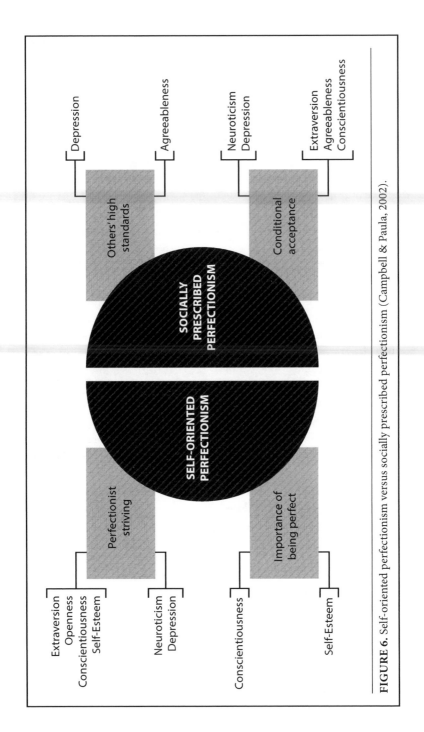

FIGURE 6. Self-oriented perfectionism versus socially prescribed perfectionism (Campbell & Paula, 2002).

selves, it's very difficult to see our way out of it. And if we are so busy trying to keep ourselves from drowning in that shame, we are in no place to find our passions or even think about persevering through the experience. All we can think about is survival and guarding ourselves from feeling that low again.

How Did My Kid Get This Way?

If I were to list out all of the times I've wondered why my kids did what they did, we would be here a while. Why did my son swallow a penny? Why did my daughter try to flush the toilet paper roll? It's normal to want to understand why our kids—these amazing, beautiful creatures—turn into people we don't recognize. Some things make no sense (Really? Flushing cardboard?), but other things have been studied by researchers to help us get to that "why."

Barrow and Moore (1983) provided us with four factors that contribute to kids becoming perfectionists:
1. their parents are too critical,
2. their parents have unreasonable expectations of them,
3. their parents don't communicate approval, and
4. their parents are perfectionists.

There you have it. But, in the spirit of grit, it doesn't really matter how we got here. What matters is how we move forward.

Overcoming Perfectionism

Cognitive behavioral therapy (CBT) is a widely used method that psychologists use when working with individuals with personality disorders (e.g., depression, anxiety) and—you guessed it—perfectionism. Essentially, it's the process of helping people cope by understanding how one's thoughts, behaviors, and emotions contribute to the disorder and identifying strategies for dealing with this triad of obstacles.

The thoughts of perfectionism can vary, but they include feelings of inadequacy and insecurity. The replaying tape in the mind of the perfectionist is saying that she is not good enough or that she is going to fail. She may also overexaggerate the results of this "failure," saying that she will never pass this class, never graduate, etc. (Antony & Swinson, 1998).

Perfectionist behaviors include procrastination or working and reworking on an assignment. Your child may be inflexible when you try to change his course and may communicate this by being defiant toward you. He may also avoid taking risks because he is afraid he will be unsuccessful. Perfectionism is also studied frequently in relation to anorexia and other behaviors that involve extreme control.

The emotions of perfectionism range from extreme highs to extreme lows. It can manifest itself in depression, anxiety, and anger. These emotions are exacerbated when one spends a lot of time and effort on something, but is still unhappy with the results.

The first step is helping your child understand how her thoughts, behaviors, and emotions contribute to her perfectionism. You and your child can talk about what each of those looks like, and you can ask her to create a list of things a perfectionist might think, do, and feel. Generating a list in a safe way will be helpful as you move on to the next step.

Perfectionism stems from a fear of failure.

The next step is more introspective. It involves some serious mindfulness, with her paying attention to when she is exhibiting perfectionistic tendencies. You could use a time journal, where every 2 hours she takes a mindful minute to pause and reflect. You could randomly text or call her to ask questions related to her thoughts, behaviors, and feelings. The point is that you get into the specifics of what is going on and when.

When addressing her thoughts, you can ask your child to look at the situation from someone else's perspective (Antony & Swinson, 1998). Oftentimes the things we tell ourselves are much harsher than what we would say to our best friend, or even a stranger. This can help you work together to identify whether her thoughts are realistic, given the situation.

Because perfectionism stems from a fear of failure, a way to treat perfectionistic behaviors is to expose her to what she fears most. She can purposefully leave a word misspelled in her essay, just to see what happens. Or walk into class unprepared. If she normally checks her math homework three times before turning it in, back it down to twice one night, and then eventually down to one check. If her perfectionism manifests itself in procrastination, help her create a realistic checklist and timelines (and have her decide how she wants to be held accountable). The point is that she will realize that the world does not implode when things do not go perfectly.

To work on her emotions around perfectionism, help her see the big picture. For example, does it really matter that she couldn't remember the Pythagorean theorem? Or who is going to remember that she tripped in the hallway? What is the worst possible thing that could happen as a result, and does that really matter? You can help her develop techniques to calm herself when she feels anxious and recognize how it feels to be able to let something go rather than dwell on it.

The Power of Reframing

Reframing is the process of taking a given situation and morphing it into something positive. For example, your child makes the junior varsity tennis team instead of varsity, and he's upset. You can reframe that to focus on the leadership role he will play on his team and the excitement that comes from turning novices into more advanced players.

Reframing begins with labels: I'm terrible at math; I can't dance. Children pick up this self-talk from the adults who surround them, particularly their parents. So if you don't want your children to label themselves with negativity, don't label yourself (or them) that way. In fact, as a parent, you play a huge role in helping your child reframe. Here's how (Alexander & Sandahl, 2016):

1. Be mindful of negative thoughts (yours and your child's).
2. Practice reframing by giving your child a statement and asking her to rewrite it into something more positive.
3. Avoid using superlatives and exaggerations, like better, worst, always, and never, in everyday language.
4. Discuss actions just as they are, not as personality traits.
5. Use humor, even when dealing with hard things.

Wait . . . My Kid Isn't a Perfectionist: Exploring Underachievement

My eighth-grade daughter came home at the end of the school year with a course guide that was more than 100 pages. I was thrilled! In high school and college (grad and undergrad), I devoured my course guides, circling classes that interested me and turning down the pages so that I could go back and carefully weigh the pros and cons of each course. My daughter, however, was not thrilled. She announced to us that she would not be taking any "hard" classes and voiced her exasperation that she was not allowed to take more than one art class each semester. I was crushed, and my husband and I had to regroup.

You see, my daughter is not motivated toward academic excellence. At times she can be an underachiever, but usually she is a "flatchiever" who does just enough. Her motivation is directly tied to her interests and has very little to do with wanting to excel or push herself. In case you also have a flatchiever living under your roof, let's try to understand why this happens.

First, let's talk about my daughter. Her main concern is connecting with her friends, so she will not do anything to jeopardize that. This means that she will not commit to anything that takes up her free time, just in case her friends have time to hang out. One issue with this is that she's waiting around while her friends are out pursuing dreams and making things happen—let me just tell you how frustrated this makes me. (And, I assure you that I have not given up on her.) The other issue is that her interests do not align with her friends' interests. Sure, they all love discussing boys, their latest Netflix obsessions, and who posted what on social media, but that's where their similarities end. Our children need friends who look and behave like them. It's simply easier for them to imagine the trajectory of their own dreams if it mirrors someone they respect. For example, if a child's peers don't value high achievement, then she will likely mirror that belief (Webb, Gore, Amend, & DeVries, 2007). Additionally, it is easier for her to not try than to try and fail, *and* she has no goals for her future. Sound familiar?

Maybe your child isn't a flatchiever like mine. Maybe he seemed like a typical kid who graduated high school, went to college, and then had the audacity to move back into your house! Let's explore some of the reasons why this could be, but let me warn you. It's complicated. Moving back home after college is not ideal, but it may be a necessity due to financial constraints or severe emotional or medical reasons. Although it's easy to forget, remember that you know your child best. You are also your child's number one in everything—number one supporter, advocate, and cheerleader. Sometimes it's absolutely necessary for your child to move back home, so know that I am not here to shame you or your child. I'm addressing the child who should be on his own, but isn't.

Underachievement can be a move of power. Perhaps your child feels controlled by your vision of what he should be doing (Webb, Gore, Amend, & DeVries, 2007). Or he doesn't know what it feels like to be intrinsically motivated to learn because he's always been so focused on the "next step" of his life. It could also be depression, a need for attention, or other psychological issues. It's complicated, remember?

Schneider (2003) categorized underachievement into six distinct types. Six! There may be reasons behind your child's behavior, and we should shift our focus from "he's just being lazy" to "he's got some issues we need to tackle." I want to explore these with you and provide some strategies for supporting your child. Before we dive in, it's important to note that sometimes getting professional help (like a counselor) is necessary. If you feel as though you've "tried everything" and your child doesn't seem to be making progress, there may be more going on. It can be incredibly beneficial to bring in an impartial person to help sort through things. Moving on . . .

Type I: The Underachiever Avoiding Responsibility

Sammy "forgets" his responsibilities, despite having the same chores for years. As he gets older, he makes excuses for his poor performance and gives up when things get too difficult. Sammy is quick to tell you about his weaknesses and seems friendly, although he shows his anger passive-aggressively.

Here's what you do: Help Sammy set realistic goals for himself and talk about the actions he is taking to achieve them. Create a time and space for Sammy to study. Perhaps from 5:00–5:30, it's homework time at your house. If

Sammy doesn't have homework, he can read, but either way you are providing him with the structure to support his achievement. He may as well just do his homework because you're going to make him work anyway. Help Sammy identify his positive attributes and make connections between how hard he works and the outcomes of that work.

Type II: The Anxious Underachiever

Sammy relies on you, his teachers, and his friends to assure him that he's worthy. He might be a perfectionist and probably puts things off until the last minute. He can identify potential obstacles, but he usually blows them way out of proportion.

Here's what you do: Help Sammy identify negative and disparaging thoughts he has of himself (when he's calmed down), and talk through those thoughts with him. Encourage him to take academic risks and positively reinforce his attempts to be independent. Sammy may also benefit from role-playing with you, so that he can practice how to assert himself and share his concerns with his teachers and other authorities. This will keep him from internalizing the anxiety until it spirals out of control.

Type III: The Underachiever Searching for Identity

Sammy is preoccupied with figuring out his place in the family, his friend group, and society. He explores some big existential questions as he struggles to figure out what he wants to do with his life. He also underachieves in some areas of his life, but not others (which rapidly increases your level of frustration with him).

Here's what you do: Spend time exploring Sammy's big questions with him. If he's willing to talk to you, you should listen. Help him turn the conversation to goals and then brainstorm potential effects of his underachievement on reaching those goals. He may benefit from journaling or participating in group activities (e.g., youth groups, clubs, etc.).

Type IV: The Underachiever With a Conduct Disorder

Sammy is distrustful of others and seems to lack empathy. He blames other people for his problems and tries to make himself feel safe by controlling others. He is manipulative and disguises his insecurity with bravado.

Here's what you do: Model empathy while correcting Sammy's inappropriate behavior. Create a safe environment for him and consider finding a counselor to help Sammy cope with his feelings.

Type V: The Underachiever With Oppositional Behavior

Sammy throws temper tantrums as a small child, but never grows out of this defiant behavior. He acts out his frustration of not being independent, yet responds negatively to guidance and authority.

Here's what you do: Don't allow yourself to be pulled into a power struggle with Sammy. Model and teach him how to communicate effectively. Provide opportunities for him to learn how to make appropriate decisions, and help him understand that his rebellious choices are signs of his dependency—not independence.

Type VI: The Underachiever Who Feels Discriminated Against

Sammy may have been victimized because he is atypical from society (i.e., not White, middle class, etc.) or because he does not conform to typical gender roles. He doubts himself in almost all areas of his life and isolates himself from others. He does not believe that he has control over his situation and that things are just done to him.

Here's what you do: Spend time with Sammy to dig deep into the times he has felt victimized and affirm his identity as positive. Help him find friends who share similar identities and values. You can also talk with Sammy about his interests and goals for the future, and then connect him with positive mentors. It will also be helpful for Sammy to understand how to communicate his feelings and stand up for himself respectfully.

Optimism and Empathy

Because perseverance, a large component of grit, involves pushing through struggles and not giving up, optimism and empathy are critical qualities to develop in your child.

Like optimism, empathy can be developed.

When I write about being optimistic, it's important to note that I'm not talking about the rose-colored glasses version of life. I want to discuss what it means to be a realistic optimist, a person who can filter out the irrelevant negative details in order to learn from the important details (Alexander & Sandahl, 2016). A realistic optimist doesn't feel the need to place experiences into boxes with labels, such as "good" or "bad." Instead, she draws meaning from both the positive and the negative, which ultimately reduces the stress and anxiety that typically accompanies struggle.

Like optimism, empathy can be developed. It begins at home, like many of our behaviors and perspectives on life. Children who are raised by authoritative parents are more likely to develop empathy. These parents allow their children to fail and experience the emotions that accompany those failures (Alexander & Sandahl, 2016). They ask questions that allow their children to explore their feelings, rather than telling them how to behave and what to think.

It is also important for parents to talk to their children about how their actions affect others and to teach them how to apologize authentically. Kids need to know how it feels when someone apologizes and when someone doesn't. They need to understand what it's like to be hurt physically and emotionally *and* need to be able to voice those feelings.

The Final Word

No one can be just like me anyway.

—P!nk

The world is a complicated place full of complex people. You happen to be raising one, living right in the vortex of him developing his personality and figuring out his likes and dislikes. That's why it likely feels like you're living in the eye of a tornado some days—and that's okay. We are right there with you making mistakes and trying to do our best. Just as perfection is a waste of time for our kids, it's also a waste of time for you. Appreciate and love your child for his quirks because there is only one of him and he needs you.

Chapter 4

Stages of Development

The best part of taking my kids to their pediatrician (aside from the torture of having to hold them down for their shots) was hearing where they ranked in comparison to their peers. Were they taller than average? Did they have an abnormally large head? There was something reassuring (and oddly exciting) about hearing that my daughter was in the 98th percentile for height. Then, as they grew up, I found myself asking my mom, my friends, and anyone who would listen, if their behavior was normal. You know, questions like, "Can your kid also watch videos of trains moving across the train tracks until you're ready to lay down across those train tracks just to make it stop?"

Although I've come to realize that "normal" is relative, I also know that there is comfort in knowing you aren't alone in this parenting journey. Although you worry that your son plays outside too much, and you really wish he would read more, there is another parent who would love her bookworm to go shoot some hoops occasionally. Social media allows us to share the curated parts of our lives, which can be disheartening if you're dealing with something that seems less than perfect at home. So, let's talk about how children develop—and what that means for their grittiness.

Psychosocial Development

Erik Erikson was a psychologist who studied personality development, focusing on how our experiences growing up influence who we become as adults (McLeod, 2018). His theory included eight stages of psychosocial development (see Figure 7).

Stage One: Trust Versus Mistrust

When infants come into the world, they don't know who to trust. They learn that they can (hopefully) depend on their parents and caregivers to attend to their needs. If their needs are consistently met, they learn to feel secure and develop a sense of hope. They know that when a problem crops up, they will be supported and cared for. On the other hand, if babies do not get their needs met, or if their care is unpredictable, they learn to be afraid and anxious when crises arise. They do not trust that anyone will help them.

We know intuitively that hope is important in our lives. If you feel something is hopeless, then you will likely give up on it. After all, what's the point in exercising if you feel like you won't be able to lose those extra pounds? Or, why would you invest in the stock market if you believe nothing good will come of it? Hope accompanies power (Duckworth, 2016), and with that comes confidence.

This confidence, this belief in ourselves, is what we need to persevere through challenges. It allows us to take ownership over our decisions and whether or not we decide to push ourselves or give up. The greater the hope, the stronger that push is going to be.

Imagine the fist pumps that were happening in my car when I heard Simon Sinek echo my thoughts on the *TED Radio Hour* podcast. Guy Roz (2015), the host, and Sinek emphasized the importance of trust by saying that it is "absolutely essential for human survival." That's huge, y'all. Sinek took it even further by telling listeners to look to the people standing on each side of us. If we look to the right and to the left, but we don't feel like we can rely completely on them, then it's likely we won't grow to accomplish anything great. *That* is how important trust is to one's success—and it starts at the very beginning of life.

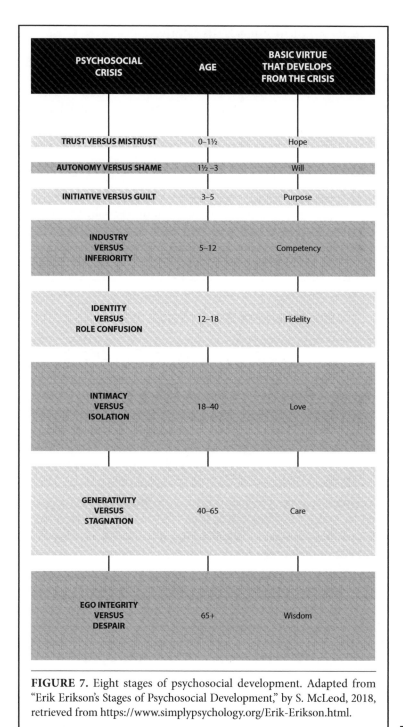

PSYCHOSOCIAL CRISIS	AGE	BASIC VIRTUE THAT DEVELOPS FROM THE CRISIS
TRUST VERSUS MISTRUST	0–1½	Hope
AUTONOMY VERSUS SHAME	1½–3	Will
INITIATIVE VERSUS GUILT	3–5	Purpose
INDUSTRY VERSUS INFERIORITY	5–12	Competency
IDENTITY VERSUS ROLE CONFUSION	12–18	Fidelity
INTIMACY VERSUS ISOLATION	18–40	Love
GENERATIVITY VERSUS STAGNATION	40–65	Care
EGO INTEGRITY VERSUS DESPAIR	65+	Wisdom

FIGURE 7. Eight stages of psychosocial development. Adapted from "Erik Erikson's Stages of Psychosocial Development," by S. McLeod, 2018, retrieved from https://www.simplypsychology.org/Erik-Erikson.html.

Stage Two: Autonomy Versus Shame

Toddlers crave independence. Once they are mobile, they love to explore on their own, running away from their parents, putting things in their mouths, and dressing themselves. This is an exhausting stage for caregivers because we have to balance our child's need for autonomy with keeping her safe.

I need to admit to something here. Before I had children, I announced that no child of mine would be waltzing through Target in a tutu and rain boots. I mean, there are standards, people. Fast forward a few years, and you would have seen me wrangling my costume-wearing toddler into one of those grocery carts that looks like a car. All of my dignity went out the window because the fight just wasn't worth it. I was tired, y'all. But, I was also doing exactly what my child needed.

The growth that accompanies failure is an important component of grit development.

By allowing our children to dress themselves, even in some crazy outfits, we are sending a big, huge message to them that their choices are valued and that they are capable of making their own decisions. Let's look at this from the other side. Imagine that you don't allow your child to choose her own outfits, and she grows up knowing that mama knows best. Or that you follow her around the playground to swoop her up if she falls down. That doesn't sound so awful, right? Well, it's a slippery slide into overdependence on you, the parent, and a drop in your child's self-efficacy. Your child soon learns that she is incapable of appropriately choosing her clothes or that taking risks (like running on the playground) will result in failure.

The growth that accompanies failure is an important component of grit development. Struggle and success are a package (Sanguras, 2017). You cannot have one without the other. To make this less painful, we need to help our kids get comfortable in their struggles so that they can experience the success of overcoming obstacles. We also want them to feel confident in their ability to succeed independently. This means that we need to encourage and allow our children to take appropriate risks as they grow up.

Stage Three: Initiative Versus Guilt

From the time our children are "threenagers" to age five, their lives revolve around play. They create storylines for their action figures and dolls. They make up games and want you to play with them. They learn how to communicate and make connections with others in this stage. If their initiatives are met with criticism or ridicule, children feel a sense of guilt and embarrassment. They receive the message that they are an annoyance to others; after receiving this message again and again, they will stop their creative play and will no longer initiate relationships with others.

Passion is a critical part of grit, and the first step in developing passion is initiating play and creating new games. We want our children to have a variety of interests when they are young, and we want at least one of those to develop into a passion. It is this passion that is exciting and keeps us pushing ourselves toward greatness. We want our children to know that we support their initiative, we value their creativity, and we believe in their ability to establish friendships with others.

There is one more point to make here. Initiative and guilt are not a dichotomy. We want our children to feel a little bit of guilt. Otherwise, they grow up believing they are the center of the universe and don't have much self-control. You know this kid—the one who interrupts his parents in the middle of their conversations, the one who insists it's always someone else's fault. We want our children to have a healthy amount of guilt and a sense of other people, so the balance of initiative and guilt is important.

Stage Four: Industry Versus Inferiority

Elementary school children become even more independent, particularly as they are influenced by their peers and teachers. They learn how to be industrious, how to get things done, and they establish beliefs about how well they can do those things. Children learn to take academic risks and—this is very important—understand the value of those risks. If their parents and teachers recognize their efforts, they will learn that trying new things is important. The pride they feel in themselves will be tied to how others perceive their efforts.

This isn't to say that we want our children to tie their self-worth to how others perceive them. They will grow out of this, but part of a child's development is making sense of how he fits in with those around him.

Another facet of this stage is the importance of raising our children to be tolerant and appreciative of others. One of my children has some quirks that aren't always appreciated by kids his age. He knows more about dinosaurs than anyone I've ever met, he does not have a competitive bone in his body, and he has a fierce desire for justice. These qualities aren't always appreciated by other third graders. There have been times he goes through recess without a friend, and he's eaten lunch on the fringes of his peer group. Those are absolutely heartbreaking moments. If my child hears that he is not valued by his peers over and over again, his sense of self will plummet and he will feel socially incompetent.

There have been times, however, when a friend has pulled my son into the group, or his teacher has asked him to share a fun fact about the Amygdalodon. This is when I am overwhelmingly thankful that he is surrounded by people who are tolerant and kind.

Stage Five: Identity Versus Role Confusion

Adolescents expend a great deal of energy on developing their senses of identity. They want to know who they are and where they fit in society. They separate themselves from their parents and identify their beliefs and values. And they are trying to figure out what they want to do with their lives.

This is a fun and exciting time for teenagers (and exhausting for their parents). Our kids push our buttons and our boundaries, but if we know what we are doing, we will appropriately nudge them back into place. It may be that your son decided that he didn't need to study for his biology exam. You have two choices. You can force him to study by making him sit with you, making flash cards and writing outlines. Or, you can let him face the natural consequences of his decision. (You probably know that I am a proponent of option two.)

If we want our kids to grow up to be gritty, we have to let them experience the consequences of their actions.

Underneath the decision to force your son to study is fear. You are afraid that he won't learn the material and will be lost on the next unit. You worry that his grade point average will drop, which will impact his class rank. You fear that he won't study and still make a decent grade on the exam. After all, what will that teach him? Step back from the situation for a moment and consider how detrimental those consequences are. If he doesn't learn the material, he will have to study in order to catch up. If his class rank drops, he will have to work harder to bring it up (if class rank even matters to him). If he still makes a decent grade on the exam, is that even in his control?

As I've said before, if we want our kids to grow up to be gritty, we have to let them experience the consequences of their actions. Sometimes the consequences are good, and other times they aren't—that really doesn't even matter. What does matter is that you send the message to your teenager that you respect and value his ability to decide for himself what is important. (Sidenote: There are definitely times when you do want to take the choices away from your son, like if he is showing signs of engaging in risky behaviors. Whenever the "natural" consequence is serious harm to himself or others, you need to just put on your parenting pants and take care of business.)

Stages six (intimacy vs. isolation), seven (generativity vs. stagnation), and eight (ego integrity vs. despair) all occur once your child enters adulthood. Healthy experiences in each of these stages lead one to develop love, care, and wisdom.

What Is Wrong With My Kid?

- "My son has no interest in getting his driver's license."
- "I can't get her to move out."
- "Why doesn't she want the freedom that comes with having her own job?"
- "What is wrong with kids today?"

It's been exciting, and very intimidating, to tell people that I'm writing a book on parenting for grit. More often than not, the response has been something like, "Thank goodness. I need to know what's wrong with my kid and how to fix him." The truth is that our kids baffle us. We, meaning everyone over 25 with a kid, don't understand why grown children/ adults don't want more independence. Sure, we try to make life uncomfortable for them by imposing curfews, eliminating their allowance, etc., and yet they still won't leave. They've taken over the basement, and there is no indication that things will change anytime soon.

I need to inform you that grit may not be the silver bullet you're looking for. But understanding grit in the context of development may provide you with some hope. After all, this would just be a sad, sad book if I ended there.

James Marcia conducted an interesting study in 1966—an oldie, but a goodie. He built it around another theory of Erik Erikson's (1956): ego identity and identity diffusion. Ego identity is the connection between a person and a social group, and it solidifies during stage five (identity vs. role confusion) that we just discussed. Identity diffusion is where things get interesting.

The truth is that our kids baffle us.

Think of a spectrum with identity achievement on one end and identity diffusion on the other (see Figure 8). Identity achievement typically occurs during early adulthood. It's when your child commits to a future career and has a firm understanding of his belief system. He may or may not be making decisions that you favor, but he is making (and following through with) his own decisions.

Identity diffusion, however, may help explain why your daughter shows no interest in getting her own apartment. She is not committed to a job, and really isn't bothered by the fact that she has no direction in her life. There may be bright moments when she bounces out the door for an interview, hoping to land her "dream job," but these quickly fade when the next opportunity presents itself. She doesn't have a strong sense of who she is and what she believes in, and can be easily swayed by an effective argument or free koozie.

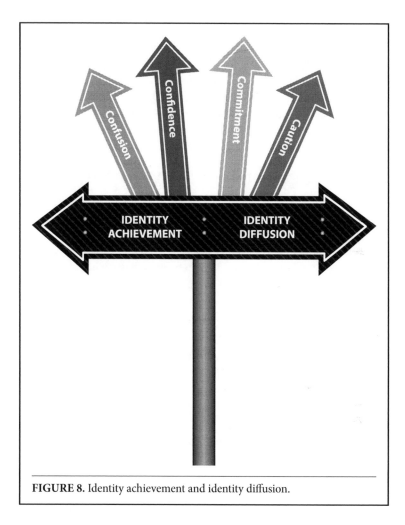

FIGURE 8. Identity achievement and identity diffusion.

Developing an Identity

Alan Waterman (1982) captured the different pieces of identity for us in a way that made sense in the 80s and still makes sense for us today. Totally rad, right? Let's break it down. To develop an identity, this is what needs to happen:

1. You are committed to a set of goals, values, and beliefs.
2. You are engaged in activities focused on those commitments.
3. You accept your strengths and shortcomings.

4. You can articulate what makes you unique.
5. You are confident in your future.

I love a great list, don't you? Now, think about those components for yourself and for your child. That will highlight the area(s) y'all need to work on (which is essentially what this book is all about).

Asynchronous Development

Asynchrony means that things are happening at different times. It's like my house during the summer, where everyone is moving in different directions. We talk about asynchronous development with gifted children who are intellectually ahead of their peers, yet lag behind socially, physically, and/or emotionally (Silverman, 2012). You can imagine the issues this can cause a kid—you remember Doogie Howser, right? And young Sheldon, from the television show with the same name.

The same is true for developing an identity. We can look to Urie Bronfenbrenner (1976) for an idea of how this can happen. Bronfenbrenner studied the influences of the systems that surround us. Beginning with the individual in the center, the closest sphere of influence is the microsystem. That extends to the mesosystem, exosystem, and macrosystem (see Figure 9).

You can imagine how the spheres of influence may get a little off-balance, depending on the situation. An adolescent boy learns about what is cool and valued by society from following the Instagram stories of his idols. A teenage girl's family is fractured by a divorce or the death of a parent. When holes are punctured in part of the ecological model, influences pour in from other areas.

By being present in your child's life and having real conversations about values and beliefs, you can smooth out the bumps in identity development. You can also ensure that your voice is one of the many sounds your child hears every day. There is nothing scarier than realizing that you are not the most important person in your child's life, but don't give up and don't leave. Be there. I promise that there is a place in your child's microsystem for you, regardless of the crazy things she says or the dumb things she does.

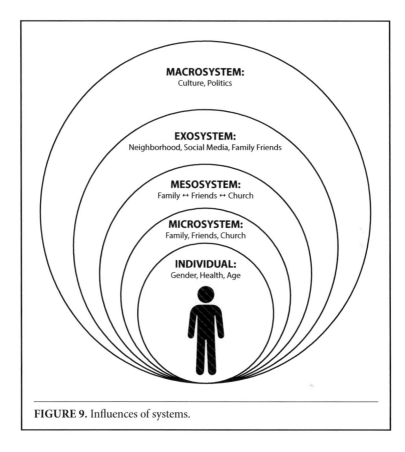

FIGURE 9. Influences of systems.

The Last Word

"Say what you wanna say
and let the words fall out
Honestly I wanna see you be brave."

—Sara Bareilles

It may seem odd to spend a chapter on your child's development when you thought you were just reading a book about grit. Well, as we know, grit is the combination of passion and perseverance. Sadly, we can't just wave a magic wand and pronounce that our kids are full of passions and that they will just tryhardergofasterdomore if we command it enough. We have to *see* them for who they are so we can help them navigate the inevitable craziness that comes with each stage of life.

Chapter 5

Self-Discipline and Self-Regulation

Before we get into a discussion of self-discipline, let's first talk about what happens when our kids mess up. It's going to happen. They will lie about where they went after school, sneak cookies at breakfast, and copy a friend's homework. And that's the best of the bad things. They might also drink alcohol at a party, bully another student, or steal from a convenience store. I'm just going to stop there because the fear spiral can get out of control really quickly when we start imagining all of the bad things.

Strategies for When Kids Push Boundaries

Because we know that it's inevitable that kids will push the boundaries, we need some solid strategies for dealing with them. One of my favorites was articulated by Foster Cline and Jim Fay (2006): "Adults must set firm, loving limits using enforceable statements without showing anger, lecturing, or using threats" (p. 57). Let's break that into pieces.

Set Firm and Loving Limits

You have a duty as a parent to provide a safe, loving, and nurturing environment where your children can thrive. You are their first teacher.

From you, they will learn how they can treat others, how they should handle conflict, and how they should view themselves. Once you step back from the minutia of your daily parenting duties, it is pretty phenomenal to realize how important you are. Whatever limits you set for your children, be sure you set them with the best of intentions—and then don't be a flip-flopper. Your word means something, and once your children realize this, you won't find yourself trapped in constant negotiations with your children. The world will thank you for this.

Whatever limits you set for your children, be sure you set them with the best of intentions— and then don't be a flip-flopper.

It's also important that you set the limits that are really important. Remember when we talked about parenting styles in Chapter 2? And how we have to be careful not to be overly controlling of our children and their environment? The same goes for setting limits. Essentially, choose your battles. You will have to let some things slide so that when you do reprimand your child, it means something and it's not just dad being a nag. Plus, it is unhealthy for children to grow up in an overly critical home (Kohn, 2005).

Use Enforceable Statements

I've been known to be a little dramatic at times. Luckily, my children chalk it up to mom being silly, but actually, I was just caught up in the moment and was grasping for some kind of control. My daughter recently reminded me that I would announce to my kitchen full of kids that if one more person left the milk out on the counter, I was going to dump the carton over his or her head. Was I really? No (mainly because then I would have to clean up the mess). But I was frustrated and said the first thing that came to my mind. Think of the consequences that you will enforce, and avoid the grandiose statements that make you look like a lunatic.

Don't show anger, lecture, or use threats. Okay, this is a tricky one. We are all human and we feel anger, sometimes really intense anger, toward our kids. That's fine, but that's when mama needs to take a breather in the bathroom to regain her composure. (After all, this is why bathrooms have doors—and locks.) There are two reasons for this tip. First, remember that your children are learning how to handle conflict by watching how you handle it. Do you want your son yelling at his future wife the way that you yell at him? Do you want your daughter to learn that the only way to get what she wants is to up the ante with threats? Second, yelling, lecturing, and threatening rarely work in the long term. The point of this whole parenting gig is to raise a good human, right? You have good intentions, but when you yell, your kid shuts down. When you lecture, your kid tunes you out. When you threaten, your kid responds out of fear. None of these responses leads us closer to our goals as parents.

Remember that your children are learning how to handle conflict by watching how you handle it.

I had a sobering moment with my fifth-grade son not too long ago. He had gotten in trouble at school for something he said to a friend. The assistant principal called me—oh, how I dread seeing the school's number pop up on my phone—and explained what happened. When I got home from work, my son avoided me. This was unusual, especially because he had been in trouble before and didn't respond this way. I kept calling his name and calling his name, to which he responded with sassy refusals to come see me. I figured out that he was scared of me. You see, my kids know that I prioritize kindness over just about everything and that I have no tolerance for bullying. And my son had just done something that very day that sounded a lot like bullying. He knew I was upset with him, and, after hugging and talking to him calmly, we talked through what happened and how he could make things up to his friend. I realized that I was doing a poor job of showing him unconditional love and that I am someone who can help him deal with his problems—even the ones he causes.

Our kids learn how to regulate themselves by how we handle it when they mess up. We are the first voice they hear and the one that their internal voice will imitate. Kohn (2005) provided us with some suggestions for how we can respond to our children:

1. **Say nothing.** Sometimes we don't have to be the judge. If our kids want our feedback, they will ask for it. Remember that we can't (and shouldn't try) to control everything.

2. **Describe what you see instead of evaluating it.** Rather than telling your son that he hurt his friend's feelings and that he needs to apologize, describe the facial expression you saw on his friend's face. This allows your son to practice empathy as he sorts through the reasons his friend may have looked sad.

3. **Invite reflection.** When your daughter refuses to clean her room, ask her why. Ask her to explain how she thinks it makes you feel when she doesn't do her chores. Rather than lecturing her, you are allowing her to use her reasoning skills to dissect the issue.

4. **Ask questions instead of passing judgment.** Find out why your son copied his friend's homework. Ask him how he felt when he cheated. Ask him if he would repeat the same decision in the future, in order to identify his threshold for dishonesty. In order for this tip to work, you really can't be judgmental. There is no room for you to say, "We don't cheat in this family" or any other family mantra.

Cline and Fay (2006) suggested that you provide your child with choices. If your 6-year-old son is throwing a temper tantrum, you ask him if he wants to walk or be carried to his room. If he continues his fit and doesn't respond, you tell him that it looks like he wants to be carried—and then you carry him to his room. If your 15-year-old daughter is having a meltdown about why you won't let her go camping with her friends without an adult, you tell her that she can communicate her frustrations by writing you a letter or you can calmly discuss it tomorrow.

By offering choices, you are setting those firm, loving limits and clearly communicating to your child what you are and are not willing to put up with. You are also giving your child control—you are setting the parameters for how this situation will end, but he has some say in it. And, you are creating a situation that you can follow through with. Sure, you might have to sit outside your son's room scrolling through Twitter to make sure he doesn't escape, or you might have to go into your room and close the door to force your daughter to make her choice. But you're doing what you said you would do. And as hard as it seems in the moment, you are doing the right thing.

The Power of Self-Discipline

Most mornings I just want my kids to exercise enough self-discipline to get ready for school without me following them around the house spewing out a litany of questions: Have you brushed your teeth? Where are your shoes? Do you want your clothes to match today? Why, oh why, do we run this routine every single day?

Beyond saving your sanity, self-discipline is crucial to a child's success. Let me tell you about a study conducted by Angela Duckworth and Martin Seligman in 2005. In phase one, they had 140 eighth-grade students complete a variety of measures related to self-control and delayed gratification. They also pulled report card grades, attendance, scores on TerraNova (a normed achievement test), and selection into a rigorous high school. In phase two, they administered similar instruments to 164 eighth graders, in addition to an IQ test, a behavioral test of delayed gratification, and questions related to study habits. The study design is really interesting, so skip the next part if you plan to read the article and don't want the findings spoiled.

Here's the deal.

1. Eighth graders who rated higher on the self-discipline scales earned higher grades, achievement scores, and were more frequently admitted to the rigorous high school than those with lower ratings.

2. Eighth graders who rated higher on the self-discipline scales had better school attendance and reported better study habits than their undisciplined peers.

3. The correlations between self-discipline and academic performance variables were stronger than the relationships between IQ and academic performance variables.

I don't know about you, but I think this is excellent news. First, IQ is fairly stable, so there isn't much that I can do to my kids to try to increase their scores on an IQ test. But, self-discipline is a learned behavior that I can absolutely influence. Do you realize what this means? For all of the things I can't control about my kids, I can help them develop self-discipline, which will likely open more doors for them academically. That's awesome, y'all.

Self-Discipline and Executive Functioning

Executive functioning is the compilation of your memory (short- and long-term), flexible thinking, and (you guessed it) self-control. Looking at these components can help us figure out what is going on with our kids and how we can help them be successful. You can even easily assess your child's executive functioning skills (see Figure 10). Executive functioning is not something we are born with, but it can be developed—this is excellent news for those of us who are reading this while also Googling how to get the macaroni out of our son's ear. There is hope!

Exercise, from running to martial arts, has been effective in increasing executive functioning skills (Davis et al., 2011; Kamijo, 2011; Tuckman & Hinkle, 1986). Isn't that amazing? Specifically, the kids involved in these studies improved in their cognitive flexibility and working memory just by moving their bodies! We've all heard about the benefits on self-discipline, but children's memories have also been shown to improve (Lakes & Hoyt, 2004).

We can take a lesson from martial arts if we want to help our children develop self-regulation. In the Lakes and Hoyt (2004) study, each martial arts class began with these three questions:

- Where am I?
- What am I doing?
- What should I be doing?

Imagine the impact that could have on your child who struggles to stay focused. By thinking about where he is, he is deliberately forcing his brain to recognize that he should focus on this moment in time. Then, he identifies what he is doing and sets a goal for what he should be doing. For example:

- Where am I? *I'm sitting at my kitchen table with my homework and snack.*
- What am I doing? *I'm eating and thinking about when I can go play my video game.*
- What should I be doing? *I should be making my list of things to do tonight. Then I should set my timer to work for 10 minutes at a time until I get my homework done.*

Your Child's Executive Functioning Skills

Directions: Place an X in the box for each area as it relates to your child's strengths and weaknesses.

Area	Weaker 1	2	3	4	5	6	7	8	9	Stronger 10
Holding Back Impulses										
Memory										
Flexible Thinking										
Focusing										
Organizing										
Time Management										
Taking Action										
Self-Motivation										
Goal Setting										

FIGURE 10. Your child's executive functioning skills assessment. From *The Impulsive, Disorganized Child: Solutions for Parenting Kids With Executive Functioning Difficulties* (p. 25), by J. W. Forgan and M. A. Richey, 2015, Waco, TX: Prufrock Press. Copyright 2015 by Prufrock Press. Reprinted with permission.

The point of this exercise is for children to focus on the present moment and to identify any gaps between what they should be doing and what they are doing. (This exercise works for adults, too!)

Stress and anxiety can inhibit a child's ability to develop executive functioning skills (Arnsten, 1998). Meditation can be a way calm a child's brain and has also been shown to improve self-control when paired with mindfulness training (Flook et al., 2010). And mindfulness training can be simple; the Flook study consisted of asking 7- to 9-year-olds to refocus themselves when their minds wandered and talking about that process. You can find guided meditations online that are designed specifically for kids. There are also apps, like Breathing Bubbles, Calm, and Headspace.

Now, as I write this, I am imagining my two little boys meditating, and I am thinking this sounds like the most painful thing ever. It's likely that one would do it, but would just be faking it—he would look calm and as though he were imagining the colors of the rainbow, when actually he would be planning his domination on his Madden 18 video game. The other would be wiggling, jiggling, and purposefully making weird noises with his breath so that he would distract us all until we just gave up.

Stress and anxiety can inhibit a child's ability to develop executive functioning skills (Arnsten, 1998).

But I can tell you from experience that it does get better. In fact, I think my boys are better at meditating than I am at this point. We started with walking meditation, where I gave them a spoonful of water and we walked outside trying not to spill the water. Once I convinced them that this was not a race, they did pretty well with it. We started with 30 seconds and then built up to several minutes. Then it was easier to move into the guided meditations—we did those at night before bed.

Additionally, establishing routines for your child can help your child develop executive functioning skills. If your morning runs the same (i.e., wake up, eat breakfast, get dressed, brush hair and teeth), then your child is less likely to need you to follow her around making sure she does what she needs to. That's what self-control is all about! It's choosing to brush your teeth when you would rather watch cartoons. It's easiest to establish routines for mornings and evenings. I've found that weekends and summers are a free-for-all, and I have to establish new routines for my children—these involve chores and other responsibilities that come before play.

Let's consider the opposite of self-control. It's being controlled by someone else (like your parents). We've discussed this in an earlier chapter in terms of parents who make every decision for their children, but there is another facet of self-control worth examining. The art of negotiation. First, let me explain what this is not. I am not talking about your son who asked for ice cream for breakfast and then continued to badger and beg you until you were ready to lose your mind. I'm talking about leaving space for your child to help with setting priorities and establishing the routines in your family. By doing this, your child gets to experience some emotional independence (which will help you in the long run) that can lead to more motivation, curiosity, and achievement (Webb et al., 2007).

Socialization is an important component to building executive functioning as well. By this, I mean that our kids need unstructured time to play. Maybe this means going to a park on a sunny day so your daughter can make some friends. Maybe you invite a friend to come over to play. The important thing is that your child learns how to interact with peers, share, and have fun in an unstructured environment. That means you're not planning out activities, spending a ton of money at the arcade, or organizing a group craft. Those things are fine occasionally, but if you care about your kid's executive functioning (and you should), then you need to back off a little.

Delaying Gratification

I was grocery shopping the other day, which is my least favorite adulting duty, and I was completely annoyed by this child I could hear in the next aisle. "Dad," the boy said. "Dad," the boy said a little louder and approximately two seconds later. "Dad," the boy yelled next. "Dad," the boy practically shouted. (It was at this point I found myself poised to hurl a box of crackers over the aisle, and I vowed to look into a grocery delivery service.) There were fewer than five seconds between each "Dad" that I could hear. This dad was clearly not answering his kid, and his kid was not having any of it. Why? What is wrong with him? Well, although kids have always been impatient, I suggest to you that today's kids are the worst.

By learning how to delay gratification, we are
more able to regulate our behaviors.

I promise I'm not going into a lecture about the spoiled offspring of Generations X, Y, or Z. But let's be real. Our kids likely cannot imagine a world without a smartphone. If they want to hear a song, they find it and play it. If they want to know how to spell a word, they type it and wait for it to autocorrect. If they want to know the weather, the time a movie starts, or when the next Taylor Swift tour starts, they can find out *right now*. They don't have to wait, and, for the most part, that's pretty awesome. Because that means we don't have to wait either, and I love some T. Swift. The difference is, though, that we grew up in a time when we had to work harder to find those answers. We regularly practiced delayed gratification because we had no choice. Our kids don't have that "luxury," so we need to devise ways for them to be able to wait before yelling "Dad" one more time.

By learning how to delay gratification, we are more able to regulate our behaviors. Do you remember that famous marshmallow study (Mischel, Shoda, & Rodriguez, 1989)? Essentially, a researcher puts a young child in a room with a marshmallow and tells the child that she can either eat it now or wait and she will be given two marshmallows. This same experiment is repeated with toys, two cookies versus five pretzels, etc. (I do question the reasoning behind the cookies vs. pretzels decision. I understand that she gets more pretzels if she waits, but I'm sure that I would simply prefer the two cookies, which would just reward me for the instant gratification. Just a thought.) The "treat" is inconsequential. What is important is that these researchers went back to the same kids 10 years later and found that the ones who delayed their gratification in the experiment were better at resisting temptations than their peers. Their parents also described them as having higher reasoning and coping skills than others. This experiment was the beginning of our focus on gratification and what it means to wait.

The key to delaying gratification is how we perceive the "prize" at the end. If one marshmallow is good, two is great, right? But what happens when we talk about cheating on a test? Picture your sweet teenage son who has rarely broken a rule and has a solid group of friends. It's a Thursday, and he wants to go cheer on his high school soccer team, but he also has a test on Friday for which he needs to study. Although he's never done it, he has some buddies who have figured out how to use their cell phones to cheat during class. They've never been caught, so he thinks the risk is minimal, and the reward of getting to hang out with his friends and get a good grade is pretty high. Plus, he's just going to cheat this one time. . . .

Although we can talk with our kids openly about the effects of cheating, the importance of honesty, etc., that may not be enough. It may not work for your daughter when she is offered marijuana. It may not work for you when you are offered a donut while trying to eat "clean." We are smart people, and we understand the consequences of giving in to temptation, but still.

We need to reconstrue how we think about this temptation. Magen and Gross (2007) tested this theory of cognitive reconstrual. They asked participants to hold a hand gripper—the official name is a hand dynamometer, but I'm picturing those hand grippers that were popular in the 80s—for as long as possible. The researchers divided the sample in half and suggested to one group that the activity was about measuring self-control and to the other group that it was about willpower. The group who believed this to be a test of willpower (as opposed to self-control) squeezed the hand gripper longer than the other group.

Begin by thinking about yourself. What are the temptations that you face, and what is it that pushes you to avoid them?

They conducted a second experiment to see if their finding would generalize to a different situation with a different sample. College students were placed in a room with a computer and a television. They first watched 5 minutes of a documentary about a national park followed by 5 minutes of a comedy show. Then, they were asked to complete a timed math test on the computer; if they earned a certain score on the test, they would be given $10. Once they started the test, the television began playing more clips from the comedy show, and researchers observed to see if the students would focus on the test or turn their attention to the TV. Part of the way through the test, half of the participants were reminded that they needed to earn a high score on the test to get their $10. The other participants were informed that the TV was a test of their willpower and challenged them to avoid looking at it while taking the test. Well, guess what? The group that was told it was a test of willpower performed better than the other group. (Also, all participants were given $10 at the end.)

The point of this study is that even if you offer a reward at the end (e.g., $10, getting an easy A by cheating, etc.), we may be more likely to exercise self-control if we shift our thinking a little. Instead of thinking that the $10 would be nice to have, we place more value on our willpower (or another characteristic that is highly regarded). The tricky part, of course, is figuring out what that is—for some, it may be willpower or respect or confidence. For others, it may be tied to cultural and familial values. And, to make things even more complicated, what works at one point with one task may not always work. Sure, you may squeeze the hand gripper today because you want to demonstrate your supreme willpower, but tomorrow you might squeeze it because you want the respect of the people watching you.

I suggest that you begin by thinking about yourself. What are the temptations that you face, and what is it that pushes you to avoid them? How has that changed over time? How does it feel when you either give in or overcome them? Once you can identify this in yourself, you are better equipped to facilitate self-control in your children. Have these same conversations with them, asking age-appropriate questions. You can even try the marshmallow test on them as a way to open the dialogue about temptation and delayed gratification.

Staying Calm and Reducing Anxiety

There is a tranquility that takes over when you are in control of your behavior. Wouldn't it be great if our kids could experience this same sense of calmness? While we continue discussing strategies, I also want to highlight two important areas for improvement.

1. **Nutrition.** Fonseca (2017) argued that emotional health is absolutely tied to what we feed our bodies. She suggested that we (kids included) steer clear of processed food, refined sugar, and caffeine if we are concerned with anxiety. Today, more than any other time, it is so easy to eat healthy. Corner markets carry organic foods, pasta can be made out of just about any vege-

table, and Amazon will deliver fresh groceries to you. It's also easy to just give in to your kid when she wants candy for her afterschool snack or she wants to buy the processed "chicken" nuggets from the school cafeteria for lunch. I'm telling you right now, for your child's physical and mental well-being, this is a fight worth fighting. If you aren't knowledgeable about nutrition, make Google your best friend. Recent online searches found on my computer include "healthy food for kids," "cheap healthy meals," and "nutritious dinners for picky eaters" (as well as "quick getaways for moms" and "how to get your kids to leave you alone for 5 minutes").

2. **Sleep.** Think about how you felt the last time you didn't get a good night's sleep. If you're like me, it's easy to remember because it was last night. How patient were you with your spouse, coworkers, and children? How focused were you on your personal and work goals? How prepared were you for all of the activities of the day? You probably had seen better days. Well now, imagine you are your child. You are a third-grade boy struggling to make friends or a hormonal teenager convinced that the world revolves around her. It's nearly impossible to navigate these difficult situations if sleep is an issue. In fact, a teen who is not getting enough sleep is more likely to experience depression and anxiety than one who is (Patruthi et. al, 2016). So, how do you handle this? Well, you set bedtimes for your kids (even the teenagers), and you stick to them as much as possible. You don't allow your child to use technology the hour before bedtime. And (my kids are not a fan of this one) you don't allow your children to take their technology to bed. You see, our bodies become attuned to the vibrations of a new text message or the audio signal that someone "loved" an Instagram post. That means that although our minds have shut down for the evening, the rest of us is alert to the signals from our phone or tablet. This seriously inhibits the quality of sleep, which affects so many areas of our lives.

Goal Setting

Another way to encourage dialogue is to talk about goals with your children—more than just the "What do you want to be when you grow up?" Sure, that's a great place to start, but you can also introduce the concept of end goals and means goals. I first heard about these two types of goals from a video featuring Vishen Lakhiani, a blogger and podcaster (Life at Mindvalley, 2012).

End goals are the big, beautiful goals (Life at Mindvalley, 2012). These are the goals you will remember on your deathbed, the ones that will hopefully live on in the memories of your loved ones. End goals are things like understanding happiness, contributing to society in a meaningful way, etc.

Means goals are the goals we must achieve, according to society, family, and friends, in order to reach those end goals. Means goals are things like earning a diploma, getting a promotion at work, etc. Lakhiani (Life at Mindvalley, 2012) suggested that we get so obsessed with these means goals that we completely lose sight of our end goals. We've all heard stories about people who fight their way up the corporate ladder only to realize they don't like it up at the top. Those are means-goalers.

Lakhiani (Life at Mindvalley, 2012) believes that end goals fall into one of three buckets: experiences, growth, or contribution. And he suggests that we start there by identifying what we want to put in each bucket—and then we can focus on the means to get there. Figure 11 is an activity to do with your child. If you're the artsy type, you can take it up a notch, but just divide a piece of paper into thirds like this. Lakhiani suggested you give yourself 90 seconds for each bucket, but your child may need more time. He also said that you need not think about time and money when making these lists.

Once you have these lists made, have your child create a vision board that outlines her end goals. Hang it on the fridge or somewhere where everyone will see it regularly. Then you can start outlining means goals, creating the road map for how to help your child get from where she is now to where she wants to be.

Experiences	Growth	Contribution
What are some things you want to do in your life? Where do you want to go? What are places you want to explore? What are accomplishments you want to achieve? What kind of home, car, or pet do you want?	What are some skills you want to learn? What new habits do you want to begin? Is there a character trait you want to develop? What do you want to improve about yourself?	How do you want to contribute to the world? What kind of difference do you want to make in the lives of your family and friends? How can you give back? What will your legacy be?

FIGURE 11. Three buckets activity.

Lean Into Your Goals

Despite having a carefully planned road map, there are going to be some glitches in the system. Your kid might lose his head and do something completely dumb—this is actually highly likely, so just prepare yourself. After all, his frontal lobe (where all rational decisions are made) is basically nonexistent. Anyway, there are going to be mistakes.

There are also going to be times when your kid realizes he's been working his tail off to achieve a means goal that leads to an end goal, and he's just not cutting it. He's taking advanced courses, working a part-time job, and applying for college scholarships. He's put a lot of pressure on himself (and likely has internalized the pressure from you as well) and is struggling with anxiety and self-doubt. Well, this is the moment when you need to encourage him to look at his bicep. Metaphorically.

I once heard someone say that you're either winning or you're learning. I like that spin on the win/lose dichotomy.

You see, I enjoy working out, and I follow a variety of trainers in my quest to stay in shape. Many years ago, I heard one trainer tell me (and his thousands of other followers) to look at my bicep. He encouraged us to pay attention to our current physical shape so that we would notice our progress. He spoke to me, with my weakling muscles and tendency to avoid looking at what I didn't like, telling me to lean into my goals instead of shying away from my weaknesses. The same is true for your son who is pushing himself in a million directions. He needs to take a moment to look at the big picture, to feel good about what he has done so far, and to refocus on what is most important.

I once heard someone say that you're either winning or you're learning. I like that spin on the win/lose dichotomy, and I think it's a powerful lesson for our children to internalize. Sure, failure feels lousy (and nothing will change that), but it's completely different when you focus on what you can get out of the experience rather than just focusing on the outcome. Jiang (2005) placed these learning experiences into three categories: empathy, value, and mission.

Empathy. We all have doubts, feel overwhelmed, and fail. We can help our children understand their own feelings when they are unsuccessful, which will transfer to them understanding how other people feel after failing.

Value. There is value in resilience. I've learned a lot about myself by how I've responded to the times I've failed. Being unsuccessful is painful, especially when it's of your own doing, but taking the time to be introspective is really important. You can help your child navigate this process.

Mission. This category refers to how our failures can inform us about our ends and means goals. Perhaps our child's goals need to be revised, or we need to help her create a new road map from one point to another.

Again, failure and success are a package (Sanguras, 2017). We know this is true. To help our children deal with their inevitable failures, we need to teach them how to detach themselves from the outcomes they can't control (Jiang, 2005). As soon as they (and we) accept that we are not in charge of how things turn out—no matter how hard we try—then we will open ourselves to new opportunities and will be much happier in the long run.

The Final Word

You got to lose to know how to win.

—Aerosmith

Self-discipline and self-regulation are skills that we must help our children develop if we want them to be gritty. They need to feel confident and in control of their choices. Additionally, if they want to pursue excellence in something great, they need to be committed to that something great. Sometimes that means sacrificing and prioritizing, but that's what real life is like. The earlier you can expose your child to these realities, the more likely he or she will adapt when he or she is older.

Chapter 6

Cultivating Your Child's Passion

Passion is when you have an affinity toward an activity that you feel is valuable, and you dedicate time and energy to this activity (Vallerand et al., 2003). The origin of the word is from the Latin root *patior*, which means to endure and suffer (Murrah, 2016). Obviously the word has shifted in meaning a little since the 12th century, but we can probably think of plenty of examples of passionate, yet suffering, people. (Ahem. Vincent Van Gogh, Sylvia Plath, Avicii . . . the list is *long*.) What's interesting, though, is that the early version of passion implied that an outside force was the cause. Today's version teeters between an inside and outside force. This makes sense, right? Your interest in something can seem to have come from nowhere (e.g., "He just always seemed to love baseball."), or it can be driven from an outside influence (e.g., "Her love for art was ignited in Mr. Haye's class.) Vallerand et al. (2003) divided passion into two types: harmonious and obsessive.

Harmonious passion is the internalization of the passion into a person's identity. This passion aligns with his values and persona, and he willingly engages in activities related to this passion. Items on the Passion Scale related to harmonious passion are "This activity allows me to live a variety of experiences," and "For me it is a passion that I still manage to control" (Vallerand et al., 2003, p. 760). The harmonious passion items were positively related to items measuring concentration and challenge. And, the researchers found that individuals with harmonious passion stopped engaging in the activity once it stopped producing positive returns. For example, Cal was highly committed to basketball for 5 years and then realized he wasn't getting better and wasn't having fun anymore, so he quit.

Obsessive passion is when there are external factors (like self-esteem and social acceptance) influencing a person's commitment to an activity. The passion becomes tied to his identity, but because he is forcing its importance on himself. Items on the passion scale to measure obsessive passion are "I cannot live without it," and "I have a tough time controlling my need to do this activity" (Vallerand et al., 2003, p. 760). The obsessive passion items were positively related to items measuring shame and negative affect. And, the researchers found that people with obsessive passion couldn't stop even when it was negatively influencing other areas of their lives. For example, Cal (our basketball player) kept pushing himself in basketball to the point of taking steroids because he knew it was the only way to make his mother proud of him. Sounds a little like suffering, doesn't it?

We should explore the ways in which we can help our children cultivate their passions.

Passion has been tied to other constructs, such as "rage to master" (i.e., singular focus on one thing), intrinsic motivation (i.e., driven from within), and "flow" (i.e., the sweet spot when you're engaged and in the zone; Fredricks, Alfeld, & Eccles; 2010). So we can summarize all of this into one definition of passion: a focused, sometimes exceptionally focused, commitment to an activity that becomes part of who you are as a person.

In their study, Fredricks et al. (2010) interviewed 25 high school and college students about passion in academic and nonacademic domains. Read these statements and tell me you don't want just a pinch of this for your kid.

I'd dance all day if I could. Forget school, forget dinner, forget everything" (p. 23).

"I get my self-satisfaction out of playing, even if I'm not playing well . . . I love to play. . . . When I want to be alone I play my violin. When I'm feeling depressed I play my violin. And even when I'm . . . feeling really happy I'll play my violin and I'll feel happier" (p. 23).

"I think [science] is really neat, and I just think it is exciting to be looking at little creatures under the microscope. I just think it is really exciting and something that's . . . like not everybody else is doing this" (p. 24).

We should explore the ways in which we can help our children cultivate their passions. Remember that it is this passion for something that will allow them to push themselves beyond the challenges in order to be successful. It is absolutely critical to raising a kid with grit. The very best thing you can do is involve your child in structured, voluntary activities (i.e., extracurricular activity, youth group, etc.). The **structure** is important, particularly for those "new" to exploring this particular passion because it provides a framework for exploring it fully. Imagine that, as a new guitar player, you are more likely to learn the range and beauty of the strings in a formal class than by watching YouTube videos alone.

The **voluntary** part is also crucial. This means that as much as I loved watching my daughter play lacrosse, I just couldn't force her to continue playing. It hurt my heart, folks, to realize this. It was my idea to sign her up for lacrosse. She attended a practice, realized she had a ton of friends playing and loved it, and we joined the team. She went to all of the practices and games and even signed up for a second season. Partway through the season, the ball was passed to her and she caught it ("SHE CAUGHT IT," I screamed from the sidelines!). She passed it to a teammate who scored, and I was so excited for my girl. When we talked about the game later, she said, "Mom, I had my moment," and my heart just burst with joy for her. She had a great group of friends and a sport she loved.

Until she didn't. It wasn't long after her "moment" that she said she didn't want to play anymore. She didn't ask to quit the team midseason— she knows better—but she told me she didn't want to sign up for a third season. I was so disappointed because I loved watching her play so, so much, but I also knew that nothing positive would come from me forcing her. (Plus, this sport costs a lot of time and money.) So, although we are currently exploring possible passions for her, she is happy as long as she has friends to hang out with and a working Netflix password. Raising teenagers is hard.

Supporting Quests for Passion

Luckily we don't have to navigate this crazy parenting world alone. Katie Hurley (2015) provided us with four ways we can support our children in this quest for passion.

Know Your Kid's Interests

Figure out what your child likes and doesn't. If your daughter is not like mine and won't just tell you, then pay careful attention to what she is doing during the activity. We signed up one of my boys for soccer when he was in early elementary school. He always said he liked soccer and would ask us to sign him up each season. Well, after a few games of watching him chatting up the opposing goalie, badgering the coach about snacks, and volunteering to be subbed out, we realized soccer was not his thing. In fact, athletics are not his thing. What did we learn about him through this process? That he loves structured time for activities where it is easy for him to socialize and make friends. And snacks. He loves a good snack.

Think Outside the Box

When we drive through the car loop at our elementary school, we see signs in the grass advertising every sport imaginable, as well as Girl and Boy Scouts. That's pretty much it. But don't forget to pay attention to your middle schooler who loves playing with LEGOs, cooking with you, or tinkering with musical instruments. Those interests can point you in directions that are different from the norm.

Nurture Optimism

The voice in our head is the loudest of them all, so begin programming your child's voice as early as possible. Focus on successes related to the process of doing something, not the product. Talk about times you have struggled and how you've worked through the negativity that crept into your head. Use every opportunity to infuse optimism into your child's spirit.

It may help to discuss what negative self-talk looks like in kids. Webb et al. (2007) provided us with four categories to consider:
1. the bad bookkeeping error,
2. the proportionality error,
3. illogical beliefs, and
4. failing to look for evidence.

The first, the bad bookkeeping error, is when your child overemphasizes the one thing that went wrong in the day, despite all of the good things. He just can't get over the mistake he made, which is where you come in. You can ask him to list the events of the day and rank them, or have him assign a value he would pay to repeat each of those events. The point is to help give him some perspective and a few strategies to help get him past the obsession.

We need to encourage our children to look for evidence to support or refute their self-talk.

The proportionality error refers to the amount of time we spend telling ourselves negative things in proportion to positive. For some children, more than three quarters of the self-talk they hear is negative. Can you imagine if you spent three quarters of your time with your child, belittling and putting her down? It's unacceptable, right? You can help your child see this by asking her if she would tell her best friend the things she tells herself. If the answer is no, then it is probably best to reframe the talk. You can help her realize the importance of having a positive self-concept.

Illogical beliefs are unreasonable and make no sense to most of us. These are statements like, "Everyone should like me," or "Life is just unfair." Again, this is when you come in. (Are you exhausted yet?) You hopefully know that everyone doesn't like you, so talk to your kids about it. You also know that, although unfair things happen sometimes, there are pieces of our lives that we can control. Talk about it.

Finally, we need to encourage our children to look for evidence to support or refute their self-talk. Failing to look for evidence just makes the illogical belief seem real. We can talk ourselves into anything, right? Well, we need to teach our kids to use this power for good. If they say that everyone should like them, ask if they like everyone. And then break the argument down from there—not to show their faults, but to reframe their self-talk.

Avoid Judgment

We've talked about avoiding judgment a lot, but that's because it's very important. You see, I didn't want my daughter to continue playing lacrosse just because she knew I loved it. Not only would this lead to her feeling rejected by me (the person who is supposed to love her unconditionally) and her receiving the message that what she wants doesn't matter, but also lacrosse would quickly become something she does because I make her. You know what that means? I could end up with a daughter who has a wall full of lacrosse trophies but no idea what she loves in life.

Instead of judging, practice reflective listening (DeLisle, 2013). You can say things like, "Wow. It really seems like you love your art class. Is that right?" or "You are really dedicated to spending your time and money on this video game. Do you think you might want to do something related to gaming when you're bigger?" or "You clearly love watching mysteries with me on TV. What is it that you love about them?" By asking questions that are nonjudgmental, you can really get to the bottom of what your kid loves (or doesn't) about what he is doing. That will help point you in a direction that is helpful to him. For example, you might learn that he loves the part of art that allows him to physically create something with his hands. Or that he doesn't really like mysteries, but he values the alone time he gets with you on the couch. This is powerful stuff.

In elementary school, my class took a trip to the California Science Center. We went through the entire exhibit on space, got to peek inside a space shuttle, and learned all about what it means to be an astronaut. Once I saw the sweet sound system that was built into the shuttle, I was ready to sign up for NASA. I'm pretty sure that was all I talked about when I got home. My mom realized that my fascination with space was pretty superficial and recognized that her daughter had a taste for the finer things in life—like a big boombox.

DeLisle (2013) suggested that we plan excursions for our children in order to see which interests are kindled. These can be nature walks, visits to historic sites, participating in building activities at your local lumber store, museum visits, etc. You can ask the owner of a boutique if she would talk with you and your daughter about being an entrepreneur, or see if a local company will provide you with a behind-the-scenes tour. There are so many possibilities!

Passion is cultivated by being exposed to a gazillion possibilities.

You can also ask your child to plan the activities for your family for a day. Give him a budget and a couple of weeks to plan (Envision, 2013). Can you imagine what he will plan for you? Plus, the positive effects this will have on his confidence, organization activities, and pleasure in spending time with his family are tremendous. *And* you can tell your daughter to ask her brother when she asks, "What are our plans for today?" Then you can enjoy that second cup of coffee in peace.

One important thing is to know that you don't need to do this alone. There are mentors and experts on *everything* who are willing and excited to share their expertise with anyone who is willing. Children are natural questioners, so your job is mainly to stoke their curiosities and support them as they see where those curiosities take them.

A second important thing to know is that you don't need to wait for your child to "find" his passion. I may just throw up if I hear another commencement speech about finding and following one's passion. It's not luck or something you just stumble upon. Passion is cultivated by being exposed to a gazillion possibilities. We need to make passions and interests part of the conversations we have with our children and take the mystery out of the whole process.

Developing Relationships With Your Children

I'm a terrible parent of first and second graders. I don't like playing Barbies, make believe, or trains. I'll do it, but the smile on my face will be fake. Give me a baby, a toddler, or anyone over the age of 7 and I'm golden, but I'll pass on the others. We all have our strengths as parents, which is normal and perfectly fine. If you struggle with establishing and maintaining close relationships with your children, I want to give you some tips.

The reason? Our kids need to feel a connection to someone in this tumultuous world. They deserve to have someone (you) they can come to. Do you know what I hear when I talk with teachers about how to help struggling students? Almost every statement begins with, "As soon as I know there is a problem. . . ." Teachers want to support their students, but they are one person with more than 20 little people depending on them. You, the parent, are one person with one person depending on you. You're the first line of defense in your child's fight against isolation.

I'm going to summarize some ways that you can connect with your children. Ideally this will happen during a shared meal, but sometimes it has to be done in the car, which is just fine. Gail Saltz (2017) provided us with some questions we can ask our kids. Now, don't pepper these at your kid rapid-fire. Just use them as a starting point to get them talking.

1. What was something you learned today? (Notice this is *not* the "How was school?" question that almost always elicits a response of "fine" or "good" or "boring.")
2. Who did you sit with at lunch?
3. Can I tell you about something weird/crazy/interesting that happened to me? (The idea here is to get your kids to realize they are not the only ones at the table and to care about other people in the family.)
4. What makes you feel grateful today? (People, we *all* need to consider this question on the regular.)
5. How would you rate your day on a scale of 1–10? Why?
6. What was something you did well today?

The important thing is that you connect with your children regularly. Listen to them, share pieces of yourself with them, and have fun with them. When they share their feelings, validate those so that they understand they aren't alone (Sorin, 2003). You don't have to be the fixer of all of the problems. You just need to show that you are on their team.

Killing Passion

Sometimes it's also helpful to think about what *not* to do to help your child cultivate his passion. Here's a quick list. **Do not:**

1. **Favor achievement over fun.** *The Washington Post* reported that 70% of kids quit organized sports by the age of 13. There are myriad reasons, but it boils down to sports not being fun anymore. Kids are forced to specialize in one sport, and excelling becomes *the* goal (Miner, 2016).

2. **Assume that every temporary obsession is a passion.** Just because your 5-year-old daughter is enamored with ballet does not mean that you need to sign her up for private lessons, summer camps, and start the application process for Juilliard (Braun, 2011). Just learn how to make one of those tight buns with her hair and breathe. She will let you know if she wants more.

3. **Mistake your passions for your child's.** Our kids are little reflections of us, which can be really fun at times. But you can't force your interests onto your children. In fact, they are more likely to be successful in their passions (particularly sports and music) if they are free to pursue them as they wish (Mageau et al., 2009). That means that you may have been a football star in college, but may have to give up the dream of junior following in your footsteps. Your support for your child is imperative if he is going to be successful, but you have to check yourself before that support turns into being pushy (Webb et al., 2007). Just stay true to your intentions.

4. **Force your kid to find a passion.** You may have a teenager who refuses to explore anything of interest to her. She may be stubborn and not all that enjoyable to be around. Brown (2018) suggested that this stubbornness may be a learned behavior in response to your demands that she get off her phone/computer/television and do something productive with her life. The best thing you can do in this situation is calmly talk with your teen and devise a plan—with her input—to provide some balance in her life. Focus on what actions can be taken rather than relying on threats and punishments.

5. **Criticize your child's interests.** Perhaps your son shows an interest in ukulele, something that you don't think will amount

to anything. Or your daughter comes home one day to announce that she wants to travel the world selling her tapestries in street fairs. Well, you have a few options. You can explain to your son that his ukulele talent is not going to take him far. Or you can tell your daughter that she won't be able to sustain her lifestyle with her textile sales. These responses will likely make your children feel insignificant (Williams, 2016). Instead, spend time getting to know what it is about these interests that drives your children. Also, you need to understand that when your children reach a certain age, your guidance begins to look like judgment and can damage the relationship you have with your kids.

The Final Word

And may your limits be unknown
And may your efforts be your own.

—The Killers

Passion is often left out when discussing grit, but I cannot underscore its importance enough. Every single time you read a news story about someone and you think, "Wow, that is a gritty fellow," look carefully at his story. You will see his deep-seated interests woven throughout. And, just like everything else with parenting, you will play an active role in helping your child define his interests and then help him further turn those into passion.

Chapter 7

School and You

It's time for some real talk, people. Teachers work long, hard hours. They didn't go into education for any nefarious reason—they make very little money because they believe in the power of education, love kids, and want to make a difference in the world. They are also imperfect and will make mistakes. They will obsess over those mistakes long after you've forgotten them and will spend their summers learning how to not repeat them.

Some teachers won't make it. They will burn out, partly because of the pressure of testing, the stress of long days with few breaks, and you. You, the well-meaning parent who loves your kid so much that you're reading a book to help you parent him better. You.

I heard someone describe parenting as though your heart is living on the outside of your body. So you might be wondering how you are supposed to balance the need to protect your child, your heart, with the desire for her to grow up to be independent. Or, what should you do when your child is struggling to meet the expectations in a class? The short answer is that you have to back off to let her live, struggle, and grow. But don't fear—there's a long answer, too!

I was a cheerleader in high school and college. Because of my size and seeming fearlessness, I was a flyer, the one who was tossed around by the other cheerleaders. A memory from one my college practices stands out very clearly. I was working with three really strong men on basket tosses. They would create a platform with their hands, I would jump up and place my toes on their hands, and they would toss me in the air. We had done this a million times, but were ready to step things up. This time

I would be tossed straight up and pull myself into a back tuck while in the air. They would catch me in a cradle-like position. That was the plan.

I remember standing there, prepped and ready. I told myself that I could do this. I also told myself that, even if we couldn't nail this basket toss, I wasn't going to die. So I jumped in, they tossed me, and I pulled my knees into my chest to start the rotation. Then I stalled out and came down head first. One of the men caught me in what looked like an upside-down bear hug. He flipped me onto my feet, we took some deep breaths, and tried again. And we nailed it again and again. (It occurred to me much later that my reassuring thought that I couldn't die doing this stunt was not entirely true.)

The reason I tell you this story is because it illustrates your role as a parent. You are the men in my basket toss story. You are the one who tosses your child into the air toward her dreams and goals. You are the one who moves underneath her, never taking your eyes off of her. You are the one who catches her, regardless of how she comes back to you.

What Should Happen in School

Let's begin by thinking about my list of 10 things we should care about in education (Sanguras, 2017; see Table 1). Then we can talk about each item on the list and what it means for you.

Learning and Demonstrating Growth

The first thing we should care about, "Children believe they can learn, and they demonstrate growth in their learning over time," is a double-barreled statement, so let's look at each piece. First of all, we want children to believe they can learn. This part absolutely begins with you. The rate of learning varies based on the person and the task, but we don't want children going through life thinking they cannot learn certain things.

Children are born with a certain amount of fearlessness and an overwhelming level of confidence. They don't even know that failure is a possibility; this is something they pick up through their experiences and interactions with others. There is absolutely nothing wrong with your 5-, 15-, and 25-year-old who dreams of being a famous actor. That belief,

TABLE 1

10 Things We Should Care About in Education

1. Children believe they can learn and they demonstrate growth in their learning over time.
2. Children love the process of discovery so much that they lose track of time.
3. Children know how to approach a challenge and problem solve their way through it.
4. Children feel empathy and genuine respect for others.
5. Children are passionate and can articulate their passions.
6. Children understand that they control their actions and, therefore, the results of those actions.
7. Children know what it feels like to want to give up—but then they persevere through it.
8. Children establish the necessary self-discipline to achieve short- and long-term goals.
9. Children are intrinsically motivated because of their dedication to the learning process.
10. Children understand their strengths and weaknesses and that these are not fixed.

Note. From *Grit in the Classroom: Building Perseverance for Excellence in Today's Students* (p. 19), by L. Y. Sanguras, 2017, Waco, TX: Prufrock Press. Copyright 2017 by Prufrock Press. Reprinted with permission.

which looks a lot like passion, will turn an average person into someone with unreal perseverance.

The second part of the statement is that children demonstrate growth over time. If we are thinking of your child as the actor, then we want to see him improve his craft over time. We also want children who continue to achieve in school, showing that their reasoning, problem solving, and critical thinking skills are improving.

The Process of Discovery

The wave of educational trends has taken us toward inquiry, discovery, and student choice. This can be really frustrating for children (and their parents) who have been told exactly what to do by their teachers. But these changes are good! Classrooms have become small laboratories that mirror real-life problems for our students to solve, which is a fabulous environment for cultivating grit. We want our kids to be comfortable being uncomfortable, and we want them to get so engaged in their work that they lose track of time. Hopefully this will lead to them chattering about their assignments with you—take a moment to enjoy this enthusiasm, even if it's happening at the most inopportune time (like bedtime, when you're trying to use the restroom, when your boss is calling, etc.).

Classrooms have become small laboratories that mirror real-life problems for our students to solve, which is a fabulous environment for cultivating grit.

Problem-Solving Skills

Problem-solving skills are developed out of a need. When your car breaks down on the way to work or your computer crashes, you have to figure out solutions quickly. So, we want our teachers to create messy problems for our kids to attempt to solve. This means that your son may come home complaining that Mrs. Jones isn't teaching him, that she just gives him work and then wants him to figure it out. Well, if Mrs. Jones is doing her job well (and let's always give teachers the benefit of the doubt), she has equipped your son with the skills needed and is expecting him to take the intellectual leap between what he knows and how he can apply it. So when you hear your son's complaints, you need to smile a secret smile, knowing that Mrs. Jones is helping your child grow into the independent boy you want.

Empathy and Genuine Respect

Learning empathy is developmental. We are born as self-centered human beings, but it's our exposure to the lives of others that helps us grow into people who can see a situation from another person's perspective. In elementary school, teachers often use children's books to explore feelings and discuss how to be a good friend. This evolves into more mature readings and studies of historical events, and discussions of what we can learn from these. You can support this development of empathy by talking about feelings regularly at home. If you're not the "talk about feelings" type, that's okay. You can help children interpret the facial expressions of others by saying things like, "He looked really mad when he missed that basket." You can also ask your child questions about how she felt when she forgot her homework or when her teacher praised her reading ability.

Learning respect begins at home. Just like in any relationship, you are responsible for teaching others how to treat you. I may ruffle some feathers here, but I am a firm believer in respect. When I moved to Texas, I quickly adapted to the "yes ma'ams" and "no sirs" that I found endearing and urged my children to do the same. I believe that you hold the door for the people coming behind you, you look people in the eye and smile when you pass them on the street, and that you treat everyone this same way—whether they look like a Fortune 500 executive, a surly teenager, or a homeless person. So, this means that you need to correct your child when she speaks to you disrespectfully, rolls her eyes at you, or slams her bedroom door. And remember that what she does at home is what she brings into the world.

Passion

We've spent a good deal of time talking about passion and how to cultivate passion in your child. The teachers at your child's school want to support him as he tries out different interests through electives, special projects, and independent study opportunities. They also know that every activity is not going to be a home run with your child, but they work hard to help him find interest and pleasure in the process.

Self-Control

There is a great deal of power in having control of something. This is why teachers allow students to make choices, even small ones, throughout the school day—because they know their students will be more engaged if they feel part of the process instead of just having education done to them. We also want our kids to understand that they are in control of their actions. This means that when they want to deflect a situation to talk about how they have been victimized, you need to bring the conversation back to them. These talks are also really effective at helping your child develop coping skills. For example, she may learn that she needs to walk away from an argument instead of engaging in it. Or that taking deep breaths before she responds to someone buys her time to gather her thoughts.

Perseverance

I have wanted to quit something thousands of times before. The workout is too hard. I have writer's block. I can't hear someone yell "MOM" one more time. But you know why I haven't quit? The rewards at the end are too great. The payoff is worth it. There are two parts to help our kids with this one. First, we have to challenge them (and allow them to be challenged) to the point where they think it's just too hard and they just can't do it. We need to celebrate the challenges our children face without judgment and without focusing on the outcome. Talking about hard things needs to be part of our daily conversations so that our kids learn that "difficult" is normal, expected, and awesome.

I know that it's difficult to talk about our moments of weakness, but it's important that we show our kids that we are normal.

Share how it feels to want to give up with your kids. I know that it's difficult to talk about our moments of weakness, but it's important that we show our kids that we are normal. By sharing our stories, we can also help our kids learn ways to deal with their own struggles, and they will realize that a struggle is not a sign of weakness. After all, their parents are pretty incredible, and they have struggled plenty of times!

Self-Discipline

We've already talked about self-discipline and what this means for you at home. And we've talked about the importance of having short- and long-term goals (i.e., ends and means goals). You are a critical part in helping your child draw connections between what she is doing at school and how this gets her closer to her goals. The connections may be a stretch, but this is all the more reason that your child needs you. You can help her shift the "why do we have to do this?" to understanding how "this" applies to her life. You are also the supportive voice cheering her on when she wants to give up.

Intrinsic Motivation

Intrinsic motivation is tricky because we don't have a good sense of where it comes from. When we, as adults, try to identify from where our motivation stems, we likely can't articulate it. We're just motivated. Well, it's all tied to self-discipline and perseverance. We also need to talk about the dedication to the learning process. I know I've said this again and again, but our kids will benefit the most from hearing us focus on the process, not the outcome. Celebrate the good and the super ugly parts and all of the times your child didn't give up. If you continue to focus on what you want your child to do (persevere), and if you understand what your child can control (the process), then you are much more likely to see these behaviors repeated.

Understanding Strengths and Weaknesses

Understanding that we all have strengths and weaknesses should be the new norm. Strengths are easy—you praise your child for blocking a goal at a soccer game and for running all of the laps in his jog-a-thon. It feels good to have someone recognize your strengths and it often makes you want to work on those things more. Weaknesses are a little trickier. It doesn't take much for a parent's constructive feedback to be misconstrued as criticism. Depending on your child's personality, it might be more effective to ask your child what he thinks he could have done differently to prepare for his algebra test. The thread woven through these strengths and weaknesses is the understanding that neither are fixed.

You've seen the mature-aged former football star reliving his glory days in the park and throwing out his back while dodging a group of kids. He doesn't understand that his skills deteriorate without practice. You've also seen the boy who was cut from the basketball team all through middle school make the varsity team in high school. He gets that he is in control of his weaknesses. Both of these people are aware of their strengths and weaknesses, which is what we want. If we want to maintain and improve a skill, we have to practice that skill.

Responding to Your Child's School Situations

There will be plenty of opportunities for you to step in and save the day for your child when it comes to school, but I want to urge you to resist. Let's talk about some of the potential situations that may arise and what you should do about them.

If your son forgets his homework at home and asks you to bring it to school, don't. Even if he cries. Even if it's worth a zillion points. Even if this is his 10th missing assignment that will result in him having to scrub the floors of the school. You can ask him after school if he wants help coming up with a plan to remember his homework in the future. But that's it.

If your daughter procrastinates a project for her history class, do not do it for her. Don't stay up late with her. Don't write her a note to excuse her from school the following day. Don't e-mail her teacher. You can help her break the project into chunks, make a list of things to do, pour her a glass of water, and go to bed. She'll figure it out.

If your son complains that he worked really hard on his essay and his teacher gave him an unfair grade, do not contact the teacher. Role-play with your son to help him practice how to approach his teacher about his essay and his grade. Remember to emphasize the process (what he can control) and not the outcome (what he can't control). Whenever possible, support your child's independence and ability to work through issues on his own.

If your daughter makes the school volleyball team, but she isn't a starter or doesn't get a lot of playing time, do not contact the coach or principal. Do not yell at the coach from the sidelines or gossip with other parents. Do not allow your daughter to quit the team. Instead, help your daughter create a list of actions she can take to improve her skills, again focusing on what she can control and letting go of what she can't (and being an example of what a respectful adult looks like).

If your son brings home an overdue library notice and can't find the missing book, do not pay the fine without a plan for how your son will pay you back. The same is true for any other fines that are the result of his negligence. This is the ideal, albeit no fun, opportunity for your son to learn that his mistakes have consequences (and that Dad won't bail him out).

I know that we worry. We don't want our kids to get in trouble or feel badly about themselves, but you are inadvertently hurting your child by saving the day. It's important that we support and guide our children without doing everything for them.

The same is true in course selection. In middle and high school, your child will get to choose her electives. She may also get to decide if she wants to take advanced/honors courses. This is an ideal moment to talk about her goals and guide her toward making decisions that align with those. You want her to be appropriately, but not overwhelmingly, challenged.

Grades

I first came across the writing of Alfie Kohn when I was researching motivation more than a decade ago. He is very critical of the emphasis that our school system places on grades. He explains that when kids prioritize grades, they don't enjoy the learning process, they choose tasks that are easy in order to earn higher grades, and they don't practice mature thinking (2005). Who wants that for their kids? Not this lady.

Here's the deal. We've talked about emphasizing the process over the outcome, which also transfers to grades. Instead of asking your daughter what grade she made on her science exam, ask her what she's learned in science recently or ask her how she prepared for her exam. Find places in that conversation to praise her efforts. And please, stop paying her for making As on her report card.

The Final Word

You gotta be bad, you gotta be bold
You gotta be wiser, you gotta be hard
You gotta be tough, you gotta be stronger

—Des'ree

Our kids spend a great deal of time at school, and we want the lessons we're teaching them about grit to extend into the school building. School is the perfect opportunity for our children to be challenged in a safe environment and to learn the skills necessary to overcome those. It's also, hopefully, a breeding ground for new ideas. Those ideas can lead to interests and then to passions. Furthermore, remember that your children's teachers have the best of intentions and that they really, truly want your child to be successful. They are committed to helping your child maintain hope through difficult times and to cheering them on during times of stress. Even if it takes you doling out "Let's Go, Teddy" t-shirts to all of your child's teachers, remember that you're all working toward the same goal. (Also, don't really give out those shirts.)

Chapter 8

Social Grit

When my daughter was in eighth grade, I had to take her to the dentist in the middle of the day. We were driving back to school after her appointment, and she begged me to take her out to lunch. I insisted that she get back to school as soon as possible, but then she broke my heart a little. She said that she didn't really have a place to eat lunch. (I'm tearing up writing about this right now, FYI.) Her school had a rule that eight students could sit at one table, so once the table was full, the leftover kids had to find a different spot. She had always been one of the solid eight, but things were shifting. Girls were making new friends, and boys were sometimes included. All of this meant that my sweet girl was out. (You can bet that I took her to lunch after hearing this story, while I also tried to figure out how I could quit my job to eat with her everyday—as though she would want that.) She eventually found her place, and I didn't have to quit my job, thank goodness.

Our lives would be easier, and our hearts would remain intact, if we could protect our children from every force that threatened them. Because that's not the way the world works, we have to find ways to support our children as they navigate tricky social situations.

Grit implies a certain level of mental toughness—the ability to overcome obstacles to come out stronger on the other side. We've spent a great deal of time talking about grit in academic and home settings, but it's also important in the context of social situations.

So, let's begin by looking at characteristics that are important in developing friendships. First, children need to be comfortable sharing pieces of themselves with others. In return, they feel validated and understood, which helps to build self-confidence (Reis & Shaver, 1988). This obviously begins by establishing intimate relationships with parents, siblings, and close relatives. As children mature, they look to their peers for connection (Buhrmester, 1990).

> We have to find ways to support our children
> as they navigate tricky social situations.

Obviously, to have friends one has to be a friend. This means by continuing to model and support your child's development of empathy, you are helping her learn what it means to be a good friend. Another interesting component of being a good friend is the ability to show admiration for another person (Mikami, 2010). It's important that you teach your child how to give a genuine compliment (and how to receive such praise). Again, set the example for your child by showing her that you give and receive compliments with ease.

I love this summary of empathy versus sympathy delivered by Brené Brown (as cited in Jiang, 2015). Empathy nourishes connection, while sympathy does the opposite:

> When someone is in a deep hole and they shout out from the bottom and say "I'm stuck, it's dark, I'm overwhelmed." And then we look and we say "Hey" and we climb down: "I know what it's like down here and you are not alone." Sympathy is [someone saying from the top] "Ooh! It's bad, huh? You want a sandwich?" (pp. 174–175).

In order to maintain friendships (and just be good people), we need our kids to understand how to be empathetic.

Mikami (2010) described children who are successful in making and keeping friends as having a "spirit of equality," meaning that they equitably handle conflict and they play fair (p. 185). You can nurture these qualities by handling conflict in your home fairly. Play games with your child, and don't let her win. Yep, you heard me. You don't need to crush her, but play with fairness.

In Chapter 6, we talked about the importance of finding structured, organized activities for your children to explore their interests. Well, it turns out that, although these activities are great for cultivating passion, they aren't so great for cultivating friendships (Ladd & Hart, 1992). The best way for you to nurture potential friendships is by organizing play-dates for your children (Frankel & Myatt, 2003). Remember that your job here is to provide the opportunity for friendships to develop, not to run an afterschool enrichment program. So put away those markers and glitter, Martha Stewart.

When my son was in third grade, I met with his teacher about some issues he was having in school. He seemed to be experiencing a lot of anxiety at school. He came home and talked about how he wanted to be homeschooled and how he didn't have any friends at school. (And, yes, my heart broke again.) Teachers described him as wandering around the playground at recess, asking if he could join different groups of kids. According him, they said they already had enough people, or they said he could join them, but then excluded him. (Again, I was ready to quit my job so that I could be at recess every day.)

Your job here is to provide the opportunity
for friendships to develop.

So, guess what we did? We asked him whom he liked hanging out with at school, and we invited those boys over to play with him. There were only two, so it was completely manageable, and they only needed us for snacks. Our son's confidence in forming and maintaining friendships has soared, and he hasn't asked to be homeschooled in quite some time. In fact, he recently had his first sleepover! I will take every parenting win, even the small ones.

When your children are young, a playdate may just be coplaying in the same room. You might observe your son and his friend playing with their toy cars, not communicating at all, and yet they will beg to see each other again to play soon. That's how it works, folks, so set another date.

When they're older, these playdates turn into "hanging out" and often involve a shared preference for an activity like walking around the mall, playing at the park, or riding bikes. You can help facilitate these for your child if your help is needed (like my son in the example above). You will walk the line to be sure you aren't being overly pushy so that your child relies solely on you for social interaction.

Bad Influences

Raise your hand if your parents told you that you could not hang out with a certain friend or crowd because they were perceived as "a bad influence." Raise your hand if you swore to your parents they were completely wrong and just didn't understand your friend like you did. Yeah, both of my hands are in the air, too. I'm sorry to tell you that your parents did the right thing. (Please don't tell my parents, though.)

This isn't to say that the boy you were not allowed to date didn't grow up to be a perfectly respectable human. It's that research suggests that 13- to 14-year-olds who engage in deviant behavior with their friends (i.e., rule breaking) are at a pretty high risk of engaging in alcohol and drug use when they are 15–16 (Dishion, Capaldi, Spracklen, & Li, 1995). Teenagers are highly influenced by their peers and are also more likely to seek peer groups with similar interests and priorities. It's a cycle, you see, and you are within your rights and responsibilities as a parent to try to break that cycle. Tell your kids that I said so—I'm sure that will help.

The Art of the "No"

Let's face it. We have a limited amount of time for everything we want to do. And if we really want to excel at something (and want our kids to do the same), we need to teach them to prioritize and turn down opportunities that distract from their goals. Before we dive in, I want to make something clear: I am not advocating that you don't let your 10-year-old play multiple sports because he needs to focus on one. I'm certainly not suggesting that your daughter has no free time because you have scheduled her to practice violin 10 hours a week. If he or she loves it, okay then. But if he or she is like a typical kid, then let him or her explore and have fun.

I feel like I've talked about this a hundred times already, but parenting is complicated. There is no right or wrong answer. It comes down to you knowing your kid and figuring out where to push and where to back off.

But there comes a time in all of our lives when we need to say, "No," and we need to teach our kids to do the same. Saying "no" is nothing to be worried about or ashamed of. It's a sign of being able to prioritize one thing over something else. It also conveys a level of confidence that we want our kids to have.

Once your child has a sense of what is important to her, it's time to talk about the activities that will lead her closer to her goals. It's also time to talk about how to say no without apologizing. This is key to developing the passions we want our children to have as they grow up.

Making Friends

Let's talk about some strategies for helping your child make friends. This can begin as conversations when your child is little, and then you can continue to refer to this list when you notice he or she is struggling. Webb et al. (2007) provided several ways you can support your child in establishing friendships.

1. **Teach your child to be a good host.** This may seem like an odd tip, but I've seen this work. When inviting someone over to play, especially a new someone, we want to teach our kids to make him feel comfortable. Teach your son to pay attention to his friend's needs—if he seems hungry, offer a snack, or if he is bored, try playing a new activity. He should also learn to walk his friend to the door when he leaves, thanking him for coming over, rather than just sending him downstairs by himself (where the strange adult-folk are).

2. **Help your child understand the difference between sharing information and bragging.** This is tricky, but everyone your child encounters will thank you for this one. If your daughter doesn't know when she's bragging, all you have to do is provide her with some scenarios and ask her if she notices sharing or bragging.

3. **Give your child advice for how to handle teasing, bullying, and peer pressure.** If your son is hungry for friends, he may put up with being teased beyond a comfortable level. This is a great opportunity to talk about the costs one should be willing to pay for a relationship. Again, you can ask him questions like, "Do you think it's okay for a friend to call another friend names?" and see what he says. From there, you can explore options for how to handle it if this happens.

Social Skills

Once our kids have friends, we want to keep them, right? Some kids will pick up on social skills through modeling, while others will need explicit details. You will know which side your kid falls on the first time you see him in public at a social event.

It might be helpful for you to teach your daughter how to introduce herself to people of all ages (Fertig, 2009). You also might want to practice how to listen and knowing when to talk, in addition to how to include others in a conversation.

We may assume that kids will just learn how to eat with their mouths closed or how to talk on the telephone, but they won't. For the longest time, and sometimes still, this is how phone conversations go with my teenage daughter. She will call me, and I will answer, "Hello." She will respond, "Hello," even though everyone knows she is supposed to say, "Hi," and then explain why she called so the conversation can move forward. So then there is this weird pause where I'm wondering who called whom and what happens now. It's awkward. So now we practice how to talk on the phone, just like we practice how to leave a good tip for a server at a restaurant, how to accept a compliment, and how to politely decline a request for a date.

The Last Word

Find out what we're made of
when we are called to help our friends in need

—Bruno Mars

As I write this book, there are daily debates on gun laws and pleas for "something to be done" to prevent more school shootings. We are living in a world that has more to offer our kids than ever before, but it can also be an isolating, lonely, and cruel place. Emotions of children are extreme, and our kids are unprepared to deal with the ramifications of their emotionally driven actions. This is why we must raise our kids to have a gentle mix of empathy, industriousness, and grit. When we sit around the dinner table talking about school with our kids, we must also address social issues so that we are oaks for our kids to lean on in times of need.

Chapter 9

Modeling Grit

Adulting is hard. There are bills, more responsibilities than time, and relationships that can make you question your sanity. It takes some serious grit to take care of business day after day, so you already know what passion and perseverance feel like.

I've mentioned several times throughout this book how important it is to model the behavior you want to see in your child. You've also heard it before in the form of public service announcements. For example, if you don't want your child to text and drive, then you don't text and drive. If you want your child to have road rage, then absolutely lose it on the next person who cuts you off on the highway. Interesting things happen when we model behavior because our little (and big) people are always watching us. . . .

Beginning at around 18 months of age, children will imitate their parents, seemingly without much thought (Nielsen & Tomaselli, 2010). In fact, children will mimic the actions of adults, even if they don't make sense. In their study, Nielsen and Tomaselli (2010) showed a group of children how to open a wooden box to get the toy inside. The adult who demonstrated the process infused actions that were irrelevant to opening the box, and the children consistently repeated all of the actions—even the ones that were unnecessary.

One theory is that kids copy adults because they don't fully understand the cause-effect relationship. For all they know, spinning around in a circle has just as much to do with opening a box as opening the latch. They trust adults and believe that if they are choosing to perform an action, then it must be necessary to the process. This is called overimitation, and researchers suggest that it may transfer across cultures and genders (Nielsen & Tomaselli, 2010). What's interesting is that chimpanzees are better equipped to prioritize behavior and only repeat the actions of their elders that immediately lead to the desired outcome (Tomasello, 1996). (That doesn't have anything to do with this chapter, but it's a fun fact you can share at your next dinner party.)

Gritty parents lead to gritty kids.

One of the texts I read in preparing for this book was *The Danish Way of Parenting* (Alexander & Sandahl, 2016). Denmark has repeatedly been ranked as the happiest country in the world, so the authors wanted to examine how the Danes may be different from others. They had a theory that happy parents led to happy kids, and then the happiness continued to spread from there. Well, I have a theory that the same is true for grit. Gritty parents lead to gritty kids.

So, this is the moment when you need to be introspective and really consider the kind of person you want your child to grow up to be. You may be thinking that you want all kinds of things for your child, many of which you don't have. Perhaps you want your daughter to graduate college, but you never attended school beyond high school. Or you want your son to have a strong faith, even though yours is a little shaky. Well, I have good news for you! You don't have to *be* everything you want your kids to be. You just need to be willing to work toward those things.

So, first things first. How gritty are you? Start by taking Angela Duckworth's Grit Scale (https://angeladuckworth.com/grit-scale). There are 10 statements that you will answer, and then you will receive a grit score. Reading the statements and reviewing your score will give you a good idea of where you stand. I encourage you to discuss the statements and share your score with your older children. From there, you know what to do because you've read this far into a book about cultivating grit in your child.

What Does Modeling Look Like?

Modeling means that you need to be an authentic, real person. Kohn (2005) suggested that we balance being the PIC (Parent in Charge) with being a human who makes mistakes. Share with your children age-appropriate details about who you are and what you like and don't like. If you don't like kale, but are committed to a healthy lifestyle, share that. When you get frustrated at work, instead of talking about it with your partner outside of your kid's earshot, include her in the discussion.

When we hide our feelings, we are teaching our kids to do the same (Alexander & Sandahl, 2016). They learn to be self-deceptive and that their feelings are unimportant, which can affect how they feel about themselves and whether they feel isolated from the people who love them. It also perpetuates the myth that everyone else has it easy or that your child is weird if he is feeling a certain way. It's no secret that kids are perceptive, so if your son asks you if something is wrong (and something is), talk about how you're feeling and share appropriate details. This humanizes you and creates a bond that will remain when your son is struggling and needs to talk.

> Our kids need to know how to genuinely give and accept an apology—the most authentic way for them to learn this is by being part of that process.

Kohn (2005) explained that our children will respect us more if we are real with them. If you make a mistake that involves them, apologize. Our kids need to know how to genuinely give and accept an apology—the most authentic way for them to learn this is by being part of that process. Kohn also described that parents are torn between two opposing forces, control and connection. When we want more control, we sacrifice connection, and he says that we need to protect (and nurture) that connection with vigor.

I know, I know. Parenting is exhausting. Alexander and Sandahl (2016) suggested that *parenting* is a verb because it certainly isn't a passive activity. I suggest that it's the kind of action that's needed to row across the Atlantic Ocean or climb Mt. Everest. Not only do you need to remember the kind of praise that is best for your kids, engage them in activities to pique their interests, and a million other things, but now you have to be an actual human being. Yes, yes, you do.

Sharing stories of your childhood with your children will help in creating these connections. It's easy for our kids to think that we've always been old and uncool, which is so not true. We need to show them that we also struggled with finding a place to sit at lunch, were cut from the baseball team, and dreamed of being a movie star. Feeling isolated with your feelings is painful, particularly for a child, but you can use your experiences to show your family members that they are not alone.

Another way that you can model grit by proxy is through stories (Alexander & Sandahl, 2016). Read stories and watch movies with your children that have a variety of plot lines and endings (even endings that don't end happily ever after). These can be the starting point for conversations about how to handle disappointments and what can be learned from our experiences. Hollywood loves a hard-knocks story, so it's easy to have a discussion about passion and perseverance after just about every movie. Table 2 is a limited list to get you thinking.

Because we want our children to have the kind of grit that leads to intrinsic motivation, it's important that they don't compare themselves to others. Do you know what that means? *You* shouldn't do that either. If you feel pricks of jealousy when you think of what your neighbors have or how thin your friend is, shut it down. It's unhealthy for you, and it's really not good for your children to see. Even if you think you're hiding it, you're not.

Big Picture

Much of our active parenting duties occur while our children are still living at home with us, which is why that has been the focus of this book. However, we know that life does not end at high school graduation—thank goodness. We want so much *more* for our kids than just a diploma, and you are the very best person to show your children what this looks like.

We want our kids to be gritty in the workforce, in their volunteer duties, in their relationships. We want them to have a stronghold on who and what is important to them, and then we want to show them the way

TABLE 2

Films to Jumpstart Conversations About Grit

Passion	Evidence of Perseverance	Influences
8 Mile		
Rap	Jimmy loses in a rap battle, and his day job interferes with his ability to pursue music.	Jimmy grew up poor and witnessed abuse. He wants to escape and create a new life for himself. (*Note.* This film is for older audiences.)
Coco		
Music (guitar)	Miguel wants to follow in his idol's footsteps and be a famous musician. He faces many obstacles, including being trapped in the land of the dead, on his journey.	Miguel's family loves him, but does not support his passion for music. In the land of the dead, he meets many relatives and a new friend who give him hope for his future.
The Goonies		
Saving Their Homes	In their quest for One-Eyed Willy's treasure, a group of teenagers must outsmart the police and a family of criminals.	The Goonies are committed to one another and to saving their families' homes. They don't leave each other behind, and they never say die.
Little Miss Sunshine		
Beauty Pageantry	Olive wants to compete in the Little Miss Sunshine competition. Her family faces many obstacles on their 800-mile journey in a run-down VW bus.	Olive's family supports her, from her desire to enter the competition to her scandalous burlesque performance onstage.
The Sandlot		
Friendship	Smalls and his friends desperately want to have the most amazing summer of their lives—playing baseball, swimming, and meeting pretty girls. They have to work together to defeat "The Beast" in order to get back to the field.	The friendship of these boys is solid, and they would do anything for each other. They also benefit from the mentorship of "The Beast's" owner.

to maintain focus on those things. And guess what? You're a grownup, whether you want to be or not. You face choices every day that demonstrate your priorities. You often have to forgo the midweek poker game with your friends because you have an early morning meeting the next day. Or you may have to decide to distance yourself from a friend who has proved to be toxic in your life. I cannot stress enough the importance of sharing these experiences with your children. Believe it or not, they see your life as easy—it's time to let them in on the secret that it's not, while reassuring them that it's also pretty darn awesome.

The Last Word

You're original, cannot be replaced
if you only knew what the future holds

—Katy Perry

To close this chapter, I want to remind you of the weight you bear when it comes to raising your child. He is watching your every move and doesn't miss a word you say (unless it's about cleaning his room). If you want him to grow up with a direction in his life and with the mental toughness and hope that he can charge toward that direction, then you need to do the same. I also want to remind you that you can do everything it takes to be an amazing parent for your child. I believe in you. We all do.

References

Agencies. (2018). Addictive video game Fortnite now weaponised by weary mothers. *The Independent*. Retrieved from https://www.independent.co.uk/life-style/gadgets-and-tech/fortnite-mothers-ban-addictive-video-game-threat-children-a8358146.html

Alexander, J. J., & Sandahl, I. D. (2016). *The Danish way of parenting: What the happiest people in the world know about raising confident, capable kids*. London, England: Piatkus.

Antony, M. M., & Swinson, R. P. (1998). *When perfect isn't good enough: Strategies for coping with perfectionism*. Oakland, CA: New Harbinger.

Armsden, G. C., & Greenberg, M. T. (1987). The inventory of parent and peer attachment: Individual differences and their relationship to psychological well-being in adolescence. *Journal of Youth and Adolescence, 16*, 427–454.

Arnsten, A. F. (1998). The biology of being frazzled. *Science, 280*, 1711–1712.

Barrow, J. C., & Moore, C. A. (1983). Group interventions with perfectionistic thinking. *Journal of Counseling and Development, 61*, 612–615.

Baumrind, D. (1967). Child care practices anteceding three patterns of preschool behavior. *Genetic Psychology Monographs, 75*(1), 43–88.

Beaton, C. (2017). This is what happens to your brain when you fail . . . and how to fix it. *Psychology Today*. Retrieved from https://www.psychologytoday.com/blog/the-gen-y-guide/201705/is-what-happens-your-brain-when-you-fail

Bharanidharan, S. (2018). Rise in prevalence of anxiety among US children and adolescents: Study. *Medical Daily*. Retrieved from https://www.medicaldaily.com/rise-prevalence-anxiety-among-us-children-and-adolescents-study-423763

Blatt, S. J. (2004). *Experiences of depression: Theoretical, clinical, and research perspectives*. Washington, DC: American Psychological Association.

Braun, B. B. (2011). Finding their passion . . . really? *Huffington Post*. Retrieved from https://www.huffingtonpost.com/betsy-brown-braun/finding-their-passion-rea_b_991621.html

Bronfenbrenner, U. (1976). The experimental ecology of education. *Educational Researcher, 5*(9), 5–15.

Brown, J. D., & Dutton, K. A. (1995). The thrill of victory, the complexity of defeat: Self-esteem and people's emotional reactions to success and failure. *Journal of Personality and Social Psychology, 68*, 712–722.

Brown, N. D. (2018). *All kids have passion—yes, even yours!* [Web log post]. Retrieved from https://neildbrown.com/17-blog/z_republished/all-kids-have-passion-yes-even-yours

Buhrmester, D. (1990). Intimacy of friendship, interpersonal competence, and adjustment during preadolescence and adolescence. *Child Development, 61*, 1101–1111.

Campbell, J. D. (1990). Self-esteem and clarity of the self-concept. *Journal of Personality and Social Psychology, 64*, 538–549.

Campbell, J. D., & Paula, A. D. (2002). Perfectionistic self-beliefs: Their relation to personality and goal pursuit. In G. L. Flett & P. L. Hewitt (Eds.), *Perfectionism: Theory, research, and treatment* (pp. 181–198). Washington, DC: American Psychological Association. http://dx.doi.org/10.1037/10458-007

Chua, A. (2011a). *Battle hymn of the tiger mother*. New York, NY: Penguin.

Chua, A. (2011b). Why Chinese mothers are superior. *The Wall Street Journal*. Retrieved from https://www.wsj.com/articles/SB10001424052748704111504576059713528698754

Cialdini, R. B., Borden, R. J., Thorne, A., Walker, M. R., Freeman, S., & Sloan, L. R. (1976). Basking in reflected glory: Three (football) field studies. *Journal of Personality and Social Psychology, 34*, 366–375. http://dx.doi.org/10.1037/0022-3514.34.3.366

Cline, F., & Fay, J. (2006). *Parenting with love and logic* (Rev. ed.). Colorado Springs, CO: NavPress.

Coates, J. (2012). *The hour between dog and wolf: Risk taking, gut feelings and the biology of boom and bust.* London, England: Penguin Press.

Conroy, D. E., Willow, J. P., & Metzler, J. N. (2002). Multidimensional fear of failure measurement: The Performance Failure Appraisal Inventory. *Journal of Applied Psychology, 14,* 76–90.

Costa, P. T., & McCrae, R. R. (1992). Normal personality assessment in clinical practice: The NEO Personality Inventory. *Psychological Assessment, 4,* 5.

Cripps, K., & Zyromski, B. (2009). Adolescents' psychological well-being and perceived parental involvement: Implications for parental involvement in middle schools. *RMLE Online, 33*(4), 1–13. doi:10.1 080/19404476.2009.11462067

Darling, N. (1993). Parenting style and its correlates. *ERIC Digest.* Retrieved from https://eric.ed.gov/?id=ED427896

Davis, C. L., Tomporowski, P. D., McDowell, J. E., Austin, B. P., Miller, P. H., Yanasak, N. E., . . . Naglieri, J. A. (2011). Exercise improves executive function and achievement and alters brain activation in overweight children: A randomized controlled trial. *Health Psychology, 30,* 91–98. http://doi.org/10.1037/a0021766

Dekovic, M., & Meeus, W. (1997). Peer relations in adolescence: Effects of parenting and adolescents' self-concept. *Journal of Adolescence, 20,* 163–176. https://doi.org/10.1006/jado.1996.0074

DeLisle, J. (2013). Mining for gold: Helping your children discover their passion. *SENG.* Retrieved from http://sengifted.org/mining-for-gold-helping-your-child-discover-their-passion

Dijkstra, J. K., Cillessen, A. H. N., Lindenberg, S., & Veenstra, R. (2010). Basking in reflected glory and its limits: Why adolescents hang out with popular peers. *Journal of Research on Adolescence, 20,* 942–958. doi:10.1111/j.1532-7795.2010.00671.x

Dishion, T. J., Capaldi, D., Spracklen, K. M., & Li, F. (1995). Peer ecology of male adolescent drug use. *Development and Psychopathology, 7,* 803–824.

Duckworth, A. L. (2016). *Grit: The power of passion and perseverance.* New York, NY: Scribner.

Duckworth, A. L. (2018). *Grit scale.* Retrieved from https://angela duckworth.com/grit-scale

Duckworth, A. L., Peterson, C., Matthews, M. D., & Kelly, D. R. (2007). Grit: Perseverance and passion for long-term goals. *Journal of Personality and Social Psychology, 92,* 1087–1101.

Duckworth, A. L., & Seligman, M. E. P. (2005). Self-discipline outdoes IQ in predicting academic performance of adolescents. *Psychological Science, 16,* 939–944.

Enns, M. W., & Cox, B. J. (2002). The nature and assessment of perfectionism: A critical analysis. In G. L. Flett & P. L. Hewitt (Eds.), *Perfectionism: Theory, research, and treatment* (pp. 33–62). Washington, DC: American Psychological Association. http://dx.doi.org/10.1037/10458-002

Envision. (2013). *Cultivating passion in your child* [Web log post]. Retrieved from https://www.envisionexperience.com/blog/cultivating-passion-in-your-child

Erikson, E. H. (1956). The problem of ego identity. *Journal of the American Psychoanalytic Association, 4,* 56–121.

Fertig, C. (2009). *Raising a gifted child: A parenting success handbook.* Waco, TX: Prufrock Press.

Flook, L., Smalley, S. L., Kitil, M., Galla, J., Kaiser-Greenland, B. M., Locke, S., . . . Kasari, C. (2010). Effects of mindful awareness practices on executive functions in elementary school children. *Journal of Applied School Psychology, 26,* 70–95.

Fonseca, C. (2017). *Letting go: A girl's guide to breaking free of stress and anxiety.* Waco, TX: Prufrock Press.

Forgan, J. W., & Richey, M. A. (2015). *The impulsive, disorganized child: Solutions for parenting kids with executive functioning difficulties.* Waco, TX: Prufrock Press.

Frankel, F., & Myatt, R. (2003). *Children's friendship training.* New York, NY: Brunner-Routledge.

Fredricks, J. A., Alfeld, C., & Eccles, J. (2010). Developing and fostering passion in academic and nonacademic domains. *Gifted Child Quarterly, 54,* 18–30. doi:10.1177/0016986209352683

Free-Range Kids. (2008–2018). *Free-range kids: How to raise safe, self-reliant children (without going nuts with worry).* Retrieved from http://www.freerangekids.com

Ginott, H. G. (1988). *Between parent and teenager.* New York, NY: Avon Books.

Glasgow, K. L., Dornbusch, S. M., Troyer, L., Steinberg, L., & Ritter, P. L. (1997). Parenting styles, adolescents' attributions, and educational outcomes in nine heterogeneous high schools. *Child Development, 68,* 507–529.

Griffin, K. W., Botvin, G. J., Scheier, L. M., Diaz, T., & Miller, N. L. (2000). Parenting practices as predictors of substance use, delinquency, and aggression among urban minority youth: Moderating effects of family structure and gender. *Psychology of Addictive Behaviors, 14,* 174–184. http://dx.doi.org/10.1037/0893-164X.14.2.174

Hara, S. R., & Burke, D. J. (1998). Parent involvement: The key to improved student achievement. *School Community Journal, 8,* 9–19.

Hirschfeld, R. M. A., Klerman, G. L., Harrison, G. G., Barrett, J., Korchin, S. J., & Chodoff, P. (1977). A measure of interpersonal dependency. *Journal of Personality Assessment, 41,* 610–618. https://doi.org/10.1207/s15327752jpa4106_6

Hsu, Y., Earley, R. L., & Wolf, L. L. (2006). Modulation of aggressive behaviour by fighting experience: Mechanisms and contest outcomes. *Biological Reviews, 81,* 33–74. doi:10.1017/S146479310500686X

Hurley, K. (2015). *The happy kid handbook: How to raise joyful children in a stressful world.* New York, NY: TarcherPerigree.

Jang, K. L., Livesley, W. J., & Vernon, P. A. (1996). Heritability of the big five personality dimensions and their facets: A twin study. *Journal of Personality, 64,* 577–591.

Jiang, J. (2015). *Rejection proof: How I beat fear and became invincible through 100 days of rejection.* New York, NY: Harmony Books.

Kamijo, K., Pontifex, M. B., O'Leary, K. C., Scudder, M. R., Ting Wu, C., Castelli, D. M., & Hillman, C. H. (2011). The effects of an after-school physical activity program on working memory on preadolescent children. *Developmental Science, 14,* 1046–1058. doi:10.1111/j.1467-7687.2011.01054.x

Kapur, M. (2016) Examining productive failure, productive success, unproductive failure, and unproductive success in learning. *Educational Psychologist, 51,* 289–299. doi:10.1080/00461520.2016.1155457

Kohn, A. (2005). *Unconditional parenting: Moving from rewards and punishments to love and reason.* New York, NY: Atria.

Ladd, G. W., & Hart, C. H. (1992). Creating informal play opportunities: Are parents' and preschoolers' initiations related to children's competence with peers? *Developmental Psychology, 28,* 1179–1187.

Lakes, K. D., & Hoyt, W. T. (2004). Promoting self-regulation through school-based martial arts training. *Applied Developmental Psychology, 25,* 283–302.

Lazarus, R. S., & Folkman, S. (1984). Coping and adaptation. In W. D. Gentry (Ed.), *The handbook of behavioral medicine* (pp. 282–325). New York NY: Guilford.

Life at Mindvalley. (2012). *The 3 most important questions to ask yourself* [Video file]. Retrieved from https://www.youtube.com/watch?v=f8eU5Pc-y0g

Mageau, G. A., Vallerand, R. J., Charest, J., Salvy, S.-J., Lacaille, N., Bouffard, T., & Koestner, R. (2009). On the development of harmonious and obsessive passion: The role of autonomy support, activity specialization, and identification with the activity. *Journal of Personality, 77,* 601–645. doi:10.1111/j.1467-6494.2009.00559.x

Magen, E., & Gross, J. J. (2007). Harnessing the need for immediate gratification: Cognitive reconstrual modulates the reward value of temptations. *Emotion, 7,* 415–428.

Marcia, J. E. (1966). Development and validation of ego-identity status. *Journal of Personality and Social Psychology, 3,* 551–558.

Martinko, K. (2015). Infographic reveals the damaging effects of helicopter parenting. *TreeHugger.* Retrieved from https://www.treehugger.com/family/infographic-reveals-damaging-effects-helicopter-parenting.html

McCrae, R. R., & Costa, P. T., Jr. (1997). Personality trait structure as a human universal. *American Psychologist, 52,* 509–516.

McCrae, R. R., & Costa, P. T., Jr. (2008). The five-factor theory of personality. In O. P. John, R. W. Robins, & L. A. Pervin (Eds.), *Handbook of personality: Theory and research* (3rd ed., pp. 159–181). New York, NY: Guilford.

McLeod, S. (2018). Erik Erikson. *Simply Psychology.* Retrieved from https://www.simplypsychology.org/Erik-Erikson.html

Mikami, A. Y. (2010). The importance of friendship for youth with Attention-Deficit/Hyperactivity Disorder. *Clinical Child and Family Psychology Review, 13,* 181–198.

Miller, C. B. (2009). Yes we did! Basking in reflected glory and cutting off reflected failure in the 2008 presidential election. *Analyses of Social Issues and Public Policy, 9,* 283–296.

Mind Tools Content Team. (n.d.). SWOT analysis: Discover new opportunities, manage and eliminate threats. *Mind Tools.* Retrieved from https://www.mindtools.com/pages/article/newTMC_05.htm

Miner, J. W. (2016). Why 70 percent of kids quit sports by age 13. *The Washington Post.* Retrieved from https://www.washingtonpost.

com/news/parenting/wp/2016/06/01/why-70-percent-of-kids-quit-sports-by-age-13

Mischel, W., Shoda, Y., & Rodriguez, M.L. (1989). Delay of gratification in children. *Science, 244,* 933–938.

Murrah, A. (2016). The etymology of passion. *Owlcation.* Retrieved from https://owlcation.com/humanities/The-Etymology-of-Passion

Nielsen, M., & Tomaselli, K. (2010). Overimitation in Kalahari Bushman children and the origins of human cultural cognition. *Psychological Science, 21,* 729–736.

Odenweller, K. G., Booth-Butterfield, M., & Weber, K. (2014). Investigating helicopter parenting, family environments, and relational outcomes for millennials. *Communication Studies, 65,* 407–425.

Patruthi, S., Brooks, L. J., D'Ambrosio, C., Hall, W. A., Kotagal, S., Lloyd, R. M., . . . & Rosen, C. L. (2016). Recommended amount of sleep for pediatric populations: A consensus statement of the American Academy of Sleep Medicine. *Journal of Clinical Sleep Medicine, 12,* 785–786.

Patterson, G. R., DeBaryshe, B. D., & Ramsey, E. (1989). A developmental perspective on antisocial behavior. *American Psychologist, 44,* 329–335.

Popova, M. (2012). Why success breeds success: The science of "The Winner Effect." *Brain Pickings.* Retrieved from https://www.brain pickings.org/2012/08/09/jonh-coates-hour-between-dog-and-wolf-winner-effect

Psychology Today. (2018). *Perfectionism test.* Retrieved from https://www.psychologytoday.com/us/tests/personality/perfectionism-test

Raz, G. (Host). (2015). *Trust and consequences* [Audio file]. Retrieved from https://www.npr.org/programs/ted-radio-hour/406238794/trust-and-consequences

Reis, H. T., & Shaver, P. (1988). Intimacy as an interpersonal process. In S. Duck (Ed.), *Handbook of research in personal relationships* (pp. 367–389). London, England: Wiley.

Roosevelt, E. (1960). *You learn by living: Eleven keys for a more fulfilling life.* New York, NY: Harper & Row.

Saltz, G. (2017). How parents can help children develop their true talents. *U.S. News.* Retrieved from https://health.usnews.com/wellness/for-parents/articles/2017-08-29/how-parents-can-help-children-develop-their-true-talents

Sanguras, L. Y. (2017). *Grit in the classroom: Building perseverance for excellence in today's students*. Waco, TX: Prufrock Press.

Schneider, C. S. (2003). Overcoming underachievement. *Center for the Gifted*. Retrieved from https://www.centerforthegifted.org/cntpub_under.htm

Shaver, A. V., & Walls, R. T. (1998). Effect of Title I parent involvement on student reading and mathematics achievement. *Journal of Research & Development in Education, 31*, 90–97.

Silverman, L. K. (2012). Asynchronous development: A key to counseling the gifted. In T. L. Cross & J. R. Cross (Eds.), *Handbook for counselors serving students with gifts and talents* (pp. 261–279). Waco, TX: Prufrock Press.

Sinclair, V. G., & Wallston, K. A. (2004). The development and psychometric evaluation of the Brief Resilient Coping Scale. *Assessment, 11*, 94–101. doi:10.1177/1073191103258144

Skenazy, L. (2008). Why I let my 9-year-old ride the subway alone. *The New York Sun*. Retrieved from https://www.nysun.com/opinion/why-i-let-my-9-year-old-ride-subway-alone/73976

Sky News. (n.d.). *US school shootings: A deadly history*. Retrieved from https://news.sky.com/story/us-school-shootings-a-deadly-history-11251204

Sorin, R. (2003). Validating young children's feelings and experiences of fear. *Contemporary Issues in Early Childhood, 4*, 80–89.

Steele, C. M. (1988). The psychology of self-affirmation: Sustaining the integrity of the self. In L. Berkowitz (Ed.), *Advances in experimental social psychology* (Vol. 21, p. 261–302). New York, NY: Academic Press.

Steinberg, L., Lamborn, S. D., Dornbusch, S. M., & Darling, N. (1992). Impact of parenting practices on adolescent achievement: Authoritative parenting, school involvement, and encouragement to succeed. *Child Development, 63*, 1266–1281. https://doi.org/10.1111/j.1467-8624.1992.tb01694.x

Stoeber, J., Kempe, T., & Keogh, E. J. (2008). Facets of self-oriented and socially prescribed perfectionism and feelings of pride, shame, and guilt following success and failure. *Personality and Individual Differences, 44*, 1506–1516. https://doi.org/10.1016/j.paid.2008.01.007

Tomasello, M. (1996). Do apes ape? In C. M. Heyes & B. G. Galef, Jr. (Eds.), *Social learning in animals: The roots of culture* (pp. 319–346). San Diego, CA: Academic Press.

Tuckman, B. W., & Hinkle, J. S. (1986). An experimental study of the physical and psychological effects of aerobic exercise on schoolchildren. *Health Psychology, 5,* 197–207.

Vallerand, R. J., Blanchard, C., Mageau, G. A., Koestner, R., Ratelle, C., Leonard, M., . . . Marsolais, J. (2003). Les passions de l'ame: On obsessive and harmonious passion. *Journal of Personality and Social Psychology, 85,* 756–767.

Waterman, A. S. (1982). Identity development from adolescence to adulthood: An extension of theory and a review of research. *Developmental Psychology, 18,* 341–358. doi:10.1037/0012-1649.18.3.341

Webb, J. T., Gore, J. L., Amend, E. R., & DeVries, A. R. (2007). *A parent's guide to gifted children.* Scottsdale, AZ: Great Potential Press.

Williams, G. M. (2016). Ten ways parents destroy their children's self-esteem. *We Have Kids.* Retrieved from https://wehavekids.com/parenting/Ten-Ways-Parens-Destroy-Their-Childrens-Self-Esteem

Winch, G. (2013). 10 signs that you might have fear of failure. *Psychology Today.* Retrieved from https://www.psychologytoday.com/blog/the-squeaky-wheel/201306/10-signs-you-might-have-fear-failure

A Parenting for Grit Playlist

TITLE	ARTIST	📅	🕐
Eye of the Tiger	Survivor	1982	4:03
Not Afraid	Eminem	2010	4:08
Just Like Fire	P!nk	2016	3:35
Brave	Sara Bareilles	2013	3:40
Dream On	Aerosmith	1973	4:25
Be Still	The Killers	2012	4:35
You Gotta Be	Des'ree	1994	4:00
Count On Me	Bruno Mars	2010	3:17
Firework	Katy Perry	2010	3:48
Gettin' Jiggy Wit It	Will Smith	1997	3:47

10 songs | 40 minutes

Appendix B

Q&A: Ask Me About Grit!

Q: Can grit be taught, or is it something kids are born with? (Submitted by Alison)

A: In Chapter 3, I discuss personality traits of our kids and how much influence parents can have over them. You can think of perseverance, one important aspect of grit, as a facet of one's personality. So, although personality can be attributed to genetics, nonshared environmental factors also greatly influence our character traits. This means that you can "teach" or play a role in cultivating grit in your child! You can do this by how you describe success and how you emphasize the process over the outcome. Think of your home as a little biosphere for producing gritty kids—and make choices accordingly.

Q: Grit seems to be associated with sports, but my son is not athletic. What should I do? (Submitted by Nadi)

A: Athletes are easily associated with grit because they routinely face "failure," whether it's losing a game, not making a team, or the fatiguing of muscles. They persevere regularly because of their love of the game. But this does not mean that your kid has to be into sports to develop grit. You simply have to mimic similar experiences for your child. First, help him identify his interests. Then, find ways that he can demonstrate his commitment to this interest. Finally, ensure that there are difficult moments during the development of this interest so that he can practice pushing through his discomfort.

Q: How can I teach my child to voice his opinions? (Submitted by Charlet)

A: Raising a child with grit means that he has a strong sense of who he is. He understands his interests and knows what it feels like to struggle. This same sense of identity is what will help him stand up for himself and voice his opinions. If he recognizes who he is and what is important to him, he can distinguish between what matters and what doesn't. As a sidenote, it will also be helpful to teach him how to respectfully communicate his ideas, even if they may cause conflict.

Q: How do I balance between letting my kids be free to find their intrinsic motivation and not letting them give up on things too easily? (Submitted by Darci)

A: An important facet of grit is perseverance, which begins with commitment. For some kids, that will be playing the same musical instrument for 10 years. For others, it's attending a weekly robotics class. Or it might just be making it through a 3-hour painting workshop. The part that matters is that you place value on sticking with something, and then talk about how it feels for your kids to finish their commitments.

Q: How can I raise a kid with grit while still trying to find my own? (Submitted by Khadijah)

A: Face it. If we waited until we were experts on all things, we never would have had kids. You don't have to be perfect—you just need to try. Just like you will do with your kids, break grit into parts. How are you doing on your interests and passions, or do you need to dedicate some time to figuring out what you care about? What about perseverance? If you're a quitter, that's okay—you can change. Most importantly, you can communicate your feelings about commitment to your kids. Just like you wouldn't pretend to be an expert flute player despite having never picked up the instrument, you don't have to feign being gritty either. Learn as you go, friend, and share your journey with your kids.

Q: How can I encourage grit over stopping at "good enough?"
(Submitted by Lauren)

A: Grit is an extreme characteristic that is associated with high achievement and extraordinary levels of success. Although the behaviors that define grit can transfer from one area of life to another, this does not mean that it always will. For example, Michael Jordan exhibited grit as a basketball player and then as a baseball player. However, if he had also pursued tennis, he may not have been as gritty. He may have even been happy with playing occasionally rather than going "all in" like he had done previously. As the parent, you know the areas where your child needs to grow and where "good enough" is okay. From there, you can push or back off accordingly. (A side note on MJ: He is, without question, a basketball legend, but did not replicate his legendary status on the baseball field. We may view his baseball career as a flop, but what we think doesn't really matter. He may have defined success differently and that's his prerogative. Remember this as you view your child's successes and failures.)

Q: How can I teach grit to an older child who suffered from childhood trauma? (Submitted by Kelly)

A: If someone has experienced trauma, from abuse to divorce of parents to homelessness, she has to be given the time and resources to heal. It is imperative to recover first so the child can return to solid ground. I'm not even close to being an expert on this, but I do know that people who have overcome trauma have grit. They are survivors. Once the healing process has begun, you can move toward developing grit in other areas.

Q: Do I have to choose between parent and friend, or can I be both? (Submitted by erniea76)

A: You are the parent and always will be, even as your child grows up and your relationship evolves. If your goal is to raise a happy, healthy, and gritty child, the decisions you make about parenting should lead toward that goal. Sometimes that means you're both on the same side about a decision and everyone is happy! Other times you will disagree, but this is when you put on your parenting pants and do the right thing.

Q: How do I deal with a child who is excessively hard on herself? (Submitted by vooga)

A: Gritty people have a firm understanding of what it means to succeed. In school, success may look like writing an organized essay. In sports, you might feel successful if you can make two free throws out of 10. You will feel satisfied with your performance in both instances because your expectations of yourself are different. Your definitions of success vary as well. It's important for your children to be able to define their success so that their levels of expectations of themselves are appropriate. If your child wants to write that organized essay, but falls short, then it's time to talk about what happened. Did she rush the assignment? Was she confused about transitioning from idea to idea? Once you get in the habit of focusing on the process rather than the product, you can help her see the places where she was successful (even if she was unhappy with the outcome).

Q: My kids are teenagers. Is it too late? (Submitted by Sara)

A: It's never too late—for anything. Do you want to learn how to roller-blade? Learn French? Lose 5 pounds? As cliché as it sounds, each day is a new opportunity to start over. Thankfully, this is also true for parenting. You can start by sharing what you've learned with your child about grit and why it's important. From there, you can both reflect on your own levels of passion and perseverance and brainstorm how you can improve and hold one another accountable. The perfect time to change for the better is now.

About the Author

Laila Y. Sanguras is a former middle school teacher, which means she's an expert in managing parent loops, writing accommodations, field trip planning, and navigating the highs and lows of middle school emotions. Plus, she knows some stuff about language arts. Her interest in grit stemmed from observing her students balk at challenging activities in school, yet excel despite struggling in areas outside of school.

She also learned a lot about grit firsthand while raising her children. She and her husband have six children between them: two elementary boys, two high school girls, and two college-aged boys. From dealing with typical kid issues to navigating the sometimes-choppy waters of having a blended family, she has had countless opportunities to persevere and maintain hope.

She received her doctorate in educational psychology from the University of North Texas. It sounds boring, but really it's exciting. A storyteller at heart, she now deeply understands how she can use numbers and words to narrate our experiences.

Follow her on Twitter (@LailaSanguras) and Instagram (@laila yvette3). You can also find her on LinkedIn at https://www.linkedin.com/in/laila-sanguras.